The Power of Giving

and How It Leads to Success and Happiness

Daniel Goldhar

The Power of Giving and How It Leads to Success and Happiness

ISBN: 978-0-9880533-0-4 (pbk)
ISBN: 978-0-9880533-1-1 (eBook)

Book design by: Maureen Cutajar
www.gopublished.com

TABLE OF CONTENTS

INTRODUCTION

The "self-help" book seems to have become the most popular genre in literature. These books maintain that in order to *be* better, you must train yourself to *think* better. But they don't tell you how that's done. They don't show you how to get the intersection of Feeling Well Street and Better Road in the town of Eternal Happiness.

We read self-help books and we feel good for a while. But we don't truly incorporate their advice into our daily lives. Sometimes we catch ourselves thinking negatively and then remember that one of those books advised us to breathe when we realize we're ruminating on negative thoughts. So we take a few deep breaths and we're relieved. "That worked," we think.

But there are days when we forget to breathe, and I'm going to show you a way to improve your life that you *won't* forget and that you can easily instill in your daily life. You'll follow through with this method because not only is it easy but it also makes good sense. It's called giving, and practicing it will make you *feel* better about yourself, make you *think* better about yourself and make others feel better about you and about themselves.

When I refer to giving, I'm talking about putting something into the universe. It can be a tangible item, such as a material gift, or an intangible item, such as a compliment. Whichever the case, when we give we feel better. That's a fact. But sometimes we find it hard to give. This book will provide you with the answers to all the questions we face around the concept of giving, including:

- Why does giving make us feel good sometimes, but other times we feel taken advantage of?
- Whom should I give to?
- What amount of giving is the right amount?

If we understand the history and the science behind giving, we can understand the concept better and *believe* in it. In this book, we'll delve into the history and science and the many forms of giving that will fill your life with joy and improve the relationships with the people you share your life with. We'll also discuss how, by giving today, you can help to design your legacy and determine the way in which people remember you when you're gone.

And, of course, we'll talk about how giving leads to success. This work is titled *The Power Of Giving and How It Leads to Success and Happiness* and by success I don't mean strictly monetary success but also personal accomplishments and success with friends and loved ones. Sometimes we need to feel good about ourselves before we can become successful, and that can be achieved by giving to ourselves. By giving ourselves a new outlook on giving and a more positive attitude toward people and by having a little faith, we give ourselves hope and self-worth. And in turn, we can become more confident, happy and successful.

My father taught me that if you give to people, they will give back to you. He grew up with little money and worked hard for every dime, waking up at 5 a.m. to run a booth at a flea market at the age of 15. He had an outgoing personality, so he was a good salesman. But he also excelled at selling because he had an early start. By the time he was 25 years old, my father was the leading salesman for a well-known giftware company. He struggled somewhat in his 30s when my sister and I were born, but he has since become financially successful. There's no doubt that this is partly due to his experience and his personality, but I believe that another significant factor in his success is his understanding of the power of giving.

Even before he became successful, he gave to his friends and family. His drive wasn't fueled by his desire to lead a good lifestyle but rather by his desire to support the lifestyle he already led, which was that of a giving person. He showed me that money holds little value if you have no one to share it with. He doesn't give because he has money—he has money because he loves to give.

Early in my life I began going out of my way to give to others. I'm always the host. I love having friends and family over for dinner and drinks. Whenever I go to others' homes, I try to bring a gift of some sort. If they've just moved into to a new apartment, I get them a housewarming present. In high school, there was a group of mentally challenged students and I became friends with one of them, Arthur. Almost 10 years later, we're still friends. I take him to movies and he rewards me with his gratitude.

I've learned that whenever we give, we get something in return. Giving is an investment, be it short-term or long-term. It either makes us feel good at the moment we give or leads to reciprocation at a later time. This is why I wanted to write this book. I've seen that being a giving person leads to success and happiness, and I want to show *you*. I truly believe you can implement this life-altering concept as a result of reading this book.

Now, if you'll give me some of your time, I think you'll be happy with what you get back.

GIVING

These days, scientists conduct research on the topic of giving on a daily basis, and even businesses understand the benefits of presenting a charitable image. I suppose we could say the act of giving is catching on. But on the other hand, as I go through my life day-to-day, I can see that there are still many people who don't realize that giving is good. Many people who don't realize there's karma in giving.

By creating good karma, giving leads to success in your personal development, your relationships and your career. These dimensions of your life are all part of your gestalt, a German word meaning "form or shape." Gestalt psychology says that everything you do, everything you think and everything that has happened to you affects every part of your being. It shapes you. To harness the power of giving, it needs to become part of our gestalt—part of our being.

Giving also makes us feel good. Elizabeth Dunn and

her colleagues at the University of British Columbia published a study, "If Money Doesn't Make You Happy Then You Probably Aren't Spending it Right," [1] designed to help consumers get more out of their spending. The researchers asked the test subjects to rate their happiness, their income levels and their expenses. They found that people were happier with more money and even happier if they spent money on others, whether it was social spending, gifts or donations to charity.

They also gave a group of 46 people $5 to $20 and told them to spend it either on themselves or on others. They were then asked to rate their happiness levels, and the results indicate that those who spent on others were happier than those who spent on themselves. "Very minor alterations in spending allocations—as little as $5—may be enough to produce real gains in happiness on a given day," Dunn concluded. Whether people had millions of dollars or only a few thousand, the fact remained that giving made them feel good.

Sonja Lyubomirsky, a psychologist at the University of California, Riverside, found similar results. She had students do five acts of kindness a week over the course of six weeks, things like helping friends with their homework or donating blood—actions that made others happy at a cost to one's self. The results showed an improvement in the well being of the subjects, especially when the five acts of altruism were done in a single day.

It seems that giving is registered in our brains as investments to be cashed in later. If we give today, we assume we'll get back tomorrow. Lyubomirsky says that giving is likely to produce unexpected positive outcomes, such as a favor performed in return later. [2] If we give today, we get a sense of security that we will be protected from hardship in tougher times. We may participate in a Cure for AIDS walk, or we may wear a moustache during November as part of the fight against prostate cancer. There are times when we feel powerless against disease and we want to control it the same way we control our lives, so we give to charity.

Additional studies confirm that giving to charity makes us feel good. In one, magnetic resonance imaging showed that the reward centers in subjects' brains lighted up as a result of giving money to charity. A group of neuroscientists and economists at the

University of Oregon recruited 22 female students and placed them in MRI machines to monitor the caudate nucleus and the nucleus accumbens, regions of the brain that produce feelings of pleasure and fulfillment. Each student participated in an economic game centered on charitable giving. They first received $100 and were told that any money left at the end of the study was theirs to keep. They then learned about a number of charities that would benefit from any donations from their account and learned that the researchers would match their donations. They rated the charities on their deservedness for money and whether the charity would directly benefit them or someone they knew.

The volunteers then watched a screen as a computer program decided what to do with their money. Sometimes students could choose whether to give to a charity. Other times, the computer "taxed" their account, donating money automatically. And once in a while, money would magically appear, either in their account or in the charities' coffers.

Most subjects experienced the "warm glow" effect after voluntarily giving money; that is, their ventral medial prefrontal cortex (VMPFC) was activated when they chose to give. Some were also wired for pure altruism. In this group, the pleasure zones of their brains lighted up when the charities received money, even if the volunteers were being taxed (money was donated randomly and automatically by the computer). More surprisingly, when these subjects saw the computer randomly place money into the account of the charity, they had a stronger positive reaction than when their own funds suddenly increased. [3]

So giving makes us feel good. But how does it make other people feel about us? Another study gives us an idea. In it, a group of university students serving as line judges in a computerized tennis game were seated in a classroom and a woman wearing the university's sweater arrived late. She apologized, sat down and shared some cookies with the other students. She turned out to be one of the players, and when a number of close calls occurred during the match, the group gave her the benefit of the doubt. In other words, if the ball was sitting on the line and could have gone either way, the group granted the woman the point.

In another group, a woman wearing the sweatshirt of a rival university walked into a different classroom.

She didn't apologize for being late and didn't share the cookies she carried in her bag. Instead, she noisily ate them all herself. The very same tennis match was played, but the majority of the close calls were not granted to this woman. [4]

This study makes a strong argument that being kind and generous rather than rude and obnoxious profits you. But does this sample speak for every person in every culture? These students were all attending university, so they were probably relatively intelligent and had bright futures, but this isn't the case for everyone. How does the average person feel toward those who give? Does he become envious and jealous?

The word schaudenfraude is found in the German language and its meaning doesn't translate directly to English, but essentially it means "happiness about the misfortune of others." Different studies show that we like to sabotage those who are doing well. One, conducted at the University of British Columbia, showed that employees who felt disengaged from others tried to sabotage their colleagues by spreading rumors about them. We'll discuss how to avoid this in the business section of this book, but for now let's consider the other side of the human brain, the side that experiences joy when someone else gets hurt. [5]

In Machiavelli's famous book *The Prince*, he says you can evoke hatred by being good as well as by being bad; by being excessively generous, you can evoke jealousy in those you are not giving to. If you give to citizens in the form of protection or decreased taxation, for example, your soldiers will be upset with you and want to steal from them. On the other hand, if you give to the soldiers by allowing them to steal from the citizens, the people will despise and ultimately overthrow you. You also risk overthrow simply because giving can make you appear to be weak. Ultimately, Machiavelli concludes that it's better to be feared than to be loved but that it's worse to be hated, and he recommends giving to no one and letting everyone fear you.

Do Machiavelli's views apply today? Not all of them, of course—his book was written in 1513. But some of his points are still valid: Don't be taken advantage of; don't give so much that people become jealous of you (or one another); practice control and humility in your giving.

But contrary to Machiavelli, we do need to give, and we need to give the most to the relationships that matter most to us. During a 26-year study, psychologist and author John Gottman, PhD, discovered a key difference between marriages that succeeded and those that failed. Couples who maintain a five-to-one ratio of positive to negative interactions usually succeed. Those who fall below a one-to-one ratio usually fail. A negative interaction may be a contemptuos comment or a critical rolling of the eyes. In a negative relationship, the process that leads to divorce often looks like this: criticism leads to contempt, which leads to defensiveness, which leads to stonewalling. It becomes difficult for a couple to work out their problems, as they are blaming each other for the relationship's demise. In positive relationships couples engage in relationship-enhancing practices, making it a point to ask about each other's day, saying they love each other, hugging or kissing when they part—little things that express support and unconditional love. But there's hope even if you don't have a five-to-one ratio. Gottman suggests that couples with negative relationships can improve their relationships through therapy, avoiding divorce and forming a stronger marriage.

It's the positive and negative thoughts we form in response to daily occurrences that shape our moods. If we talk positively to ourselves, we can improve our mood and our confidence. This is why when we're having a bad day, it's so important to give ourselves enough positive accolades to tilt the ratio back to five-to-one.

When we insult someone, it takes a lot of compliments, jokes and pats on the back to reset the ratio, so you may want to bite your tongue. For married couples, this is difficult given that they share all the ups and downs of each other's life. When times gets tough, married people can get so far down the negative-comment hole that they need hundreds of positives to climb out of it.

Money is said to be one of the most common causes of divorce, but the truth is that it's really negative thoughts and attitudes that break marriages apart. While it's true that it's better to give a genuine compliment than to give a phony one, it's also better to give a phony compliment than to give none at all.

Some people have been taught that it isn't manly to give compliments. Some people have been taught that it's not good to pamper your children. But people who pamper and compliment have positive relationships. Those who don't, suffer from poor relationships. Offering kind words or actions of any kind allows you to build healthy ratios in your relationships. Why do you think it's much more pleasurable to be in the company of people who are positive rather than those who are negative?

All that being said, we need to have some negative comments in our relationships and lives in order to strike a balance. Life is best when it's hopeful and positive, but as Gottman explained in his research, the one negative interaction for every five positive ones is actually crucial to success. Conflict helps couples clear the air and work out grievances. It helps create something of a renewal when the conflict is worked out. This is also true for employee-employer relationships and our relationships with ourselves. Companies that had a 13:1 ratio of positive comments to negative were actually likely to fail. They weren't able to foresee negative turns of events because they never wanted to bring them up. This is why lawyers and accountants and doctors who sometimes warn you of things you don't want to think about are valuable. It's better to ask for advice from an expert than to pay a lot more for it later.

Every once in a while, you need to bring up the negative things in life and discuss them. Otherwise, you're either being naïve and not seeing the negative or seeing it and choosing to avoid it. Whatever the case, you need to address undesirable events or they'll come back to hurt you.

I would also suggest that the positive-to-negative ratio shapes our moods, it also applies to the give-and-take that occurs between two people. None of us want to give all the time only to receive nothing in return, so for every five times you give, you should be able to take at least once. If you give 13 times, for example, and get back only once, you're probably in a relationship that's destined to fail.

I'd like to think the world is made up of seven billion genuinely good people who all want to give, share and love, but the truth is, there are people who take and don't give despite all the evidence that taking doesn't pay. In a study conducted by Nicholas Christakis and his colleagues at Harvard University and published in the Proceedings of the National Academy of Sciences, it was concluded that those who cheat at games won't be chosen as partners again. In the study, game participants started with a certain number of points and moved from one competitor to the next from round to round with the chance to give up these points. If players gave to one another, they would become richer, but cheaters—who would get points but not give any—would become even richer. Participants were able to choose their partners as the rounds continued, and cheaters weren't chosen again. The most successful of all the participants were the ones who never cheated. Those who did cheat eventually changed their behavior and became more cooperative.

"They found that connections between two co-operators were much more likely to be maintained than links that involved a defector," the study says. "Over time, the co-operators accumulated more social connections than the defectors did. Furthermore, as they were shunned, the defectors began to change their behavior. A defector's likelihood of switching to co-operation increased with the number of players who had broken links with him in the previous round. Unlike straightforward tit-for-tat, social retaliation was having a marked effect." [6]

If we defect from social norms and decide to cheat, the word spreads like wildfire and we become labeled. People gossip, for example—before doing business with someone, we ask others about the person's character. We want to learn about him and see if he's co-operative or if he cheats. The use of gossip can be a way to determine what proper social norms are and who's practicing them. [7]

With the technology that exists today, such as telephones, computers, social media, etc., we have become a very interlinked society. Today, you're more likely to meet that French waiter who served you 10 years ago at a café in Paris than if you'd lived 100 years ago. Therefore, it pays to be seen as a giver rather than as a taker. You won't do something dishonorable and say to yourself, "Who cares? I'll never see that person again." The term *six degrees of separation* refers to the idea that through the links of just six people or fewer, we know every person in the world. If you have a bad reputation, it will catch on. Dale Carnegie once said, "You get more bees with honey," and the bees that share your world will be in your life for a long, long time.

This applies in business too. If you work in the same industry for a long period of time, you develop a reputation, and it greatly affects your ability to form new partnerships. If you're a cheat and you burn bridges, good luck getting off your island.

A Quick Synopsis of Giving and Its Evolution in Modern History

A caveman might have decided it would be wise to be kind to another caveman and give to him because he knew he might encounter him again someday, but the idea of giving as a survival mechanism and a way to thrive became more institutionalized with the rise of societies and complex civilizations. Giving evolved just like societies evolved, from the simple to the complex. Early humans would give as a way to make peace or attain protection or as a form of trade.

In the famous book called *The Gift: Forms and Functions of Exchange in Archaic Societies*, written in 1954 by Marcel-Israël Mauss (1872–1950), Mauss concludes that in early societies, giving was "laden with power." When people give, they "shift the economic, political, kinship-oriented, legal, mythological, religious, magical, practical, personal and social fabric of their society," Mauss says. [8]

Many early cultures reacted differently to receiving gifts from how we react today. The Au and the Gnau, Papau New Guinean societies studied by Mauss, didn't like receiving gifts, because they felt obligated to reciprocate. [9]"They would reject generous offers by a cultural association with gift-giving: accumulating gifts, even if unsolicited, can imply a lowered status and force the receiver into future obligations or political alliance," [10] Mauss says. They wouldn't accept a gift because they thought there was a catch.

The Au and the Gnau had a point. We can't give constantly because that's taxing, whether we're giving time, money, possessions or smiles. As studies have shown, your endorphins fire off as a result of giving, but when we realize that we've given too much, we stop giving. This is natural and it's human. If we were to give 100 percent of what we earn and help others all the time, we'd surely work ourselves to death. Even Mother Teresa had to eat.

Malcolm Gladwell says in the book *Outliers* that throughout history, approaches to giving differed across geographies (villages with hills vs. villages on plains, for example). People would either share their crops or defend their livestock depending on where they lived. [11] If you lived beside your neighbors and shared seed and crops on the plains, you were more likely to live in a "neighborly" manner and give and take with one another. If you lived in the hills of Scotland, you couldn't be so generous as to give away a sheep or any livestock, as that would put your family at risk of starvation. If someone stole another's sheep, he would be killed, and this type of punishment frightened thieves and ultimately became accepted as a just penalty. As a result, there was less giving and more fighting and killing.

How much we give and what we give is dictated by where we live, what we earn, our moods—the particulars of our lives. That said, the power of giving has always and will always be universal. Mauss said gift-giving brings honor to both the giver and the recipient and both recognize their mutual interdependence. With the actual gift comes a spirit, or *hau*. When a gift is given, a *hau* is created and in time must be returned to the giver. If the *hau* is not returned to its creator, there is a loss of honour and the recipient becomes indebted and ashamed.

The *hau* does not have to be money or a replica of the original gift. If I choose to take you out for dinner, you can return the *hau* by taking me out for dinner next time, or you can return the *hau* in the form of compliments to me, support of my goals or praise for my accomplishments. Parents constantly give to their children, and while they have no expectation that the *hau* will be returned, it's actually returned on a day-to-day basis in the form of intangibles like trust, loyalty and love. And when it comes to friends, strangers or businesses, once we create *haus*, we believe they should be returned to us.

DIFFERENT CULTURAL ATTITUDES TOWARD GIVING

In my international-marketing textbook from third-year university, [12] there was a small photo caption on the different ways of presenting gifts in different cultures. For instance, in Europe and the United States, large and expensive gifts can easily be interpreted as bribes. In the Arab world, you shouldn't give a gift to a person upon first meeting him or give a gift to a person when you're alone with him. This is also seen as bribery—as coming on too strong—especially in business relationships. Gifts should be given only to close friends. The type of gift is important, too. It should be of the best quality, and gold and silk are not to be given to men, but perfume or cologne is appreciated. You should also always receive gifts with the right hand. This dates back to the times when there was no toilet paper in the desert and when people did their morning ritual, they used their left hands and kept their right hands clean.

In Latin America, it's best to give a gift outside of business and only after a personal relationship has begun. In China, gifts are to be presented privately, not in front of others, and in some cases giving just one of something is not proper—in Chinese philosophy, pairs symbolize balance and harmony [13] in Japan, gift-giving is central to business etiquette. It's important to bring gifts on business trips or to meetings so that if you're given something, you can reciprocate. The emphasis is on the giving, not the actual gift, though expensive gifts are common. Timing is vital, too. Give at the end of your visit. Just like in China, give in pairs and in private. Also, present the gift with two hands, and as in many other cultures, in Japan you should refuse the gift at least once before accepting it.

Whatever customs are involved, we can conclude that gift-giving requires reciprocation. So when you give in business, it can sometimes seem like bribery or corruption because you're expecting something back. In business, the act of giving can translate into saying, "Here is a gift. What are you going to do for me now?" Or "Here's a watch. Now buy my products." In many cultures, this is unethical.

When someone gives you a large expensive gift, it can make you feel uncomfortable. Why is this? Because you're getting something large and expensive and you feel the need to reciprocate and it puts pressure on you. It's like an invisible credit card that needs to be paid off in some form or another. The larger the gift, the larger the giving debt. In North America, many soon-to-be sons-in-law don't like the idea of receiving a large gift from their in-laws, such as a car or a down payment on a house. They feel as if they're being controlled and are giving their power away. The idea of a dowry is for the bride to bring money into the family of the groom. This is done in many cultures, most notably India, because it theoretically links the couple together forever, which in some cultures is perceived as frighteningly permanent.

In the 11th century in Eastern Europe, if a family had no sons they would give land to a soon-to-be son-in-law in exchange for his taking of the family name. [14] This sounds like selling your soul, but we don't know the exact reasons behind such practices. Whatever they were, in Western culture today a dowry is seen as an added expense (not necessarily monetary) that a man has to imbue. This may not be a comfortable feeling because he has student loans to pay off and savings to accumulate.

We establish customs like these in our cultures to maintain order. This order has been established from years of wisdom from our ancestors. In modern-day China, it's customary for a son to give money to his parents, almost like an allowance. For a child to give to his parents as they age is part of the order of things. But in North America, the opposite is true. Giving money to your parents is viewed as an odd imbalance of nature. It's expected that grandparents will "spoil" their grandchildren if they have the means to, not the other way around. Such customs have been created based on tradition. Through trial and error, we have come to determine what will throw the balance off and what will preserve it.

IS GIVING A RELIGIOUS ACT?

If your attitude toward giving is related to the time and place in which you live, wouldn't it also be affected by the god you worship? If most traditions are based on some sort of religious affiliation, how much does the act of giving have to do with appeasing God? How much has the religion you were born into—perhaps founded more than two thousand years ago—altered the amount you give?

I'll answer these questions soon, but first I want to explore exactly what each of the major religions believes about giving. This can help us to better understand the teachings we hear in the church, the synagogue, the Buddhist temple, the mosque or any other religious center.

JUDAISM

I'm a Jew, and though I don't practice Judaism to its full extent, I have embraced many of the "good" lessons I've learned from the Old Testament and from my elders. I've learned about the virtues of giving and about being a *mensch*. I've also learned some useful tems. In Yiddish, there are several words that exemplify the Jewish religion's strong beliefs about giving, for example. Translated as "charity," the word *tzedakah* takes its origins from a Hebrew root that means "righteousness and justice."

And the term *seychel* means "to be smart or have common sense." This word meaning has nothing to do with giving, but it's often used to refer to someone who has the common sense to be a giver. Picture an old Jewish *bubi* wearing an apron and carrying a wooden spoon, with matzoh-ball soup and kasha cooking on the stove behind her. All the while she's yelling, "That Mordechai came to my house for Shabbat dinner with nothing. He has no *seychel*, just like his mother!"

Seychel sums up the Jewish attitude toward giving: People who are smart know to give. It makes sense that when one is called *thoughtful*, he's viewed as someone who gives. In the Old Testament, countless passages speak of the good of giving. Here are just a few:

It is written in the Holiness Code and in the Deuteronomic Code: "Farmers should leave the corners of their fields unharvested and they should not attempt to harvest any leftovers that were forgotten when they had harvested the majority of a field." "Olive trees should not be beaten on multiple occasions and whatever remains from the first set of beatings, should be left." "According to the Holiness Code, these things should be left for the poor and for strangers." And from Leviticus: "You shall not take vengeance or bear a grudge against your kinsfolk. Love your neighbor as yourself: I am the LORD."

Twelfth century scholar Maimonides didn't play a part in the formation of Judaism, but he did transform and improve on the way Jews interpret the Bible and how, with the help of the Torah, it leads our lives. In Medieval times, Maimonides was considered to be the face of Judaism. He was very wise and was well respected in Egypt, where he worked under the Sultan. He taught medicine, law, philosophy and theology, and most notably wrote the Mishneh Torah, which is a 14 book commentary on the Old Testament. He would help people in their day-to-day lives and give them guidance and advice about how to be good people. He said to give in the following order: first to your relatives, then to your household, then to your city and finally to other cities. He also had a hierarchy for how the act of giving guides people toward virtue. Each rung up the ladder represents a higher degree of virtue:

1. Giving money, a loan, your time or whatever else it takes to enable an individual to be self-reliant.
2. Giving cheerfully but giving too little.
3. Giving cheerfully and adequately but only after being asked.
4. Giving before you are asked.
5. Giving when you do not know who is the individual benefiting but the recipient knows your identity.
6. Giving when you know who the individual is that is benefiting but they do not know you.
7. Giving when neither you nor the recipient is aware of the other person's identity.
8. Giving begrudgingly and making the recipient feel disgraced or embarrassed.

So, yes, Jews take giving very seriously. To the very end. In Judaism, burying the deceased is the most generous deed you can do for them, because they cannot repay you. Lifting dirt and putting it on their caskets is your selfless way of sending them to the afterlife.

Christianity

Many passages in the New Testament speak highly of the act of giving. When one thinks of Christianity, giving often comes to mind. Unlike Judaism, Christianity is ecumenical, which means that it's for everyone. Jesus, its founder, did not belong to a chosen people; he had come to save everyone. We can find thousands of passages in the New Testament that describe Jesus, his followers and their feelings about giving and about being a good person, but I'll use only a few examples.

In Matthew 6:1-4, Jesus speaks about about giving anonymously. He says not to take credit for giving because God will reward you:

> Take heed that ye do not your alms (good deeds) before men, to be seen of them: otherwise ye have no reward of your Father which is in heaven. Therefore when thou doest thine alms, do not sound a trumpet before thee, as the hypocrites do in the synagogues and in the streets, that they may have glory of men. Verily I say unto you, They

> have their reward. But when thou doest alms, let not thy left hand know what thy right hand doeth: That thine alms may be in secret: and thy Father which seeth in secret himself shall reward thee openly.

Paul writes in the First Letter to the Corinthians, chapter 13 (KJV):

> Though I speak with the tongues of men and of angels, and have not charity, I am become as sounding brass, or a tinkling cymbal. And though I have the gift of prophecy, and understand all mysteries, and all knowledge; and though I have all faith, so that I could remove mountains, and have not charity, I am nothing. Charity never faileth: but whether there be prophecies, they shall fail; whether there be tongues, they shall cease; whether there be knowledge, it shall vanish away. For we know in part, and we prophesy in part. But when that which is perfect is come, then that which is in part shall be done away. When I was a child, I spoke as a child, I understood as a child, I thought as a child: but when I became a man, I put away childish things. For now we see through a glass, darkly; but then face to face: now I know in

> part; but then shall I know even as also I am known. And now abideth faith, hope, charity, these three; but the greatest of these is charity.

And in Second Corinthians 8:4 and 12 and 9:10 and 14, he writes:

> The believers considered it a privilege to give. They begged to give. Giving under pressure contradicts Grace. Even if a believer has nothing to give, it is fully accepted by God, provided there is a willing mind to give. God keeps on supplying so the believer can keep on giving. Giving also stimulates prayer, love and an admiration of Grace in the believer who gives graciously.

And in Acts 20:35, Jesus said, "It is more blessed to give than to receive."

ISLAM

Islam is the submission to the will of God. It was founded around 610 AD by a man named Muhammad. By 900 AD, in what is known today as the Middle East, nine out ten people were followers of Islam.[15]

In Islam, giving is also highly valued. The Quran says about the righteous: "They give food, out of love for Him

(Allah), to the poor, the orphan, and the slave, saying: We feed you only for Allah's pleasure—we desire from you neither reward nor thanks." Al-Insaan 76:8-9

And about righteousness (2:177):

It is not righteousness
That ye turn your faces toward East or West;
But it is righteousness -
To believe in Allah (The One and Only God)
And the Last Day
And the Angels
And the Book
And the Messengers;
To spend of your substance out of love for Him
For your kin
For orphans
For the needy
For the wayfarer
For those who ask,
And for the ransom of slaves;
To be steadfast in prayer
And practice regular charity;

> To fulfil the contracts which ye have made;
>
> And to be firm and patient in pain (or suffering) and adversity
>
> And throughout all periods of panic.
>
> Such are the people of truth the Allah-fearing (God-conscious).

A form of giving that Muslims partake in is *zakāt*, which means "purity and cleanliness." It's the giving of a fixed portion of one's wealth to charity, generally to the poor and needy. The amount given varies from 2.5 percent to 20 percent of one's income. *Zakāt* is one of the five pillars of Islam, the others being the *shahada* (creed), *salat* (daily prayers), *sawm* (fasting during Ramadan) and the *haji* (the pilgrimage to Mecca at least once in a lifetime).

Buddhism

Buddhism was founded around 460 BC, about the same time that Judaism was born. The short history of Buddhism is that it did not spread throughout China until 800 years after it was established. Like Christianity, Buddhism was ecumenical and had no written Word. So people had to interpret it from the works of its followers.

Buddhism's Noble Eightfold Path consists of the following "rights":

1) Right understanding—understanding Buddhism

2) Right intention, or right thought—having purpose and a positive outlook on the world and its issues

3) Right speech—avoiding harmful language and using kind words; avoiding the use of unkind words with others even if the situation calls for it

4) Right action:

    a) refraining from destroying living beings
    b) refraining from stealing
    c) refraining from sexual misconduct (adultery, rape)
    d) refraining from false speech (lying)
    e) abstaining from intoxicants that lead to heedlessness

5) Right livelihood—choosing an occupation or way of life that will support the other fundamentals of Buddhism

6) Right effort—making the effort to replace negative thoughts with positive ones

7) Right mindfulness—focusing on the body, emotions and mental workings

8) Right concentration—laying the framework for effective meditation

Total willingness to give is the wish-granting gem for fulfilling the hopes of wandering beings.
It is the sharpest weapon to sever the knot of stinginess.
It leads to bodhisattva conduct that enhances self-confidence and courage,
And is the basis for universal proclamation of your fame and repute.
Realizing this, the wise rely, in a healthy manner, on the outstanding path
of (being ever-willing) to offer completely their bodies, possessions, and positive potentials.
The ever-vigilant lama has practiced like that.
If you too would seek liberation,
Please cultivate yourself in the same way.

LAMA TSONG KHAPA

As you can see, Buddhism teaches that, in order for someone to find Nirvana, he must not only give but also understand the powers of giving and generosity.

Buddhist teachings focus on positive thought and mental well being, aspects of giving to one's self that I'll address in later sections. Like Christianity and Islam, Buddhism was an offshoot of a different religion. It developed out of Hinduism.

Hinduism

Hindus worship deities and divas more than Buddhists do, but both religions teach about karma, a term that people in the West often use but don't fully understand. *Karma* refers to the good or bad things that happen to people in response to their actions and words. Both Hinduism and Buddhism teach that karma is part of a system that rewards you for the good things you do and say and punishes you for the bad things you do and say. Buddhists and Hindus believe that the result of your actions in this life will flow into your next life.

Confucianism

Confucianism is one of the oldest religions practiced in China today. It was begun by Confucius around the same time as Judaism was founded. It incorporates a firm belief in giving, as evidenced by this passage: "Zi Gong asked, 'Is there one word that may serve as a rule of practice for all one's life?' The Master said, 'Is not RECIPROCITY such a word?'"

TAOISM

Laozi (Lao Tzu), who was said to be a contemporary of Confucius, founded Taoism, another ancient Chinese religious practiced today. He was the author of the Tao Te Ching, from which comes the passage "Regard your neighbor's gain as your own gain, and your neighbor's loss as your own loss." He also wrote:

Your name or your person,
which is dearer?
Your person or your goods,
Which is worth more?
Gain or loss,
Which is a greater bane?
Excessive stinginess
Is sure to lead to great expense;
Too much store
Is sure to end in immense loss.
Knowing contentment
You will suffer no humiliation;
Knowing when to stop
You will be free from danger;
You will thereby endure.

Truthful words are not beautiful; beautiful words are not truthful.

He who knows has no wide leaning he has no wide learning does not know.

He who is good does not have much; he who has much is not good.

The sage has no hoard. Having bestowed all he has on other, he has yet more; having given all he has to others, he is richer still.

Hence the way of heaven does not harm but benefits; the way of man does not contend but is bountiful.

As we can see, Lao Tzu's words were very simple yet profound.

How It All Started

If we return to the times when religions were formed and see what was taking place politically and economically, we can see how people were either benefiting from giving or feeling the need for it. If we return to 3100 BCE, for example, we see that the richest place in the world was Egypt, and the ruling Pharaohs' regime was based on a give-and-take relationship, which involved the aristocrats and the peasants. The people paid homage to the Pharaoh because he had a divinity to the gods. As centuries passed, people continued to worship their kings, their dictators and their Pharaohs because they were perceived to be closest to the gods. This system worked because it was based on the illusion of the divinity of those in power and the belief that they could improve the lives of the people. But as time went on, people began to realize that these "gods" were not real. They began to realize that nature was chaotic and unpredictable and that it was their responsibility to make their own destinies. As a result, the illusion of divinity collapsed.

Karl Jaspers, a German philosopher, called the centuries surrounding 500 BC the *Axial Age* because they formed an axis around which history turned. In the Axial Age, man came into being, and writings of the time included Confucian, Taoist, Buddhist and Jain documents, Greek philosophy and the Hebrew bible. These writings gave people a guide to life and to its meaning.

The Axial Age grew out of a time when trade and commerce were developing in and among small states. From shipwrecks discovered in the Mediterranean Sea, archaeologists have determined that the number of ships docking in the Mediterranean in the 6th century BC was far higher than in any period before. Not only were goods changing hands, but ideas were flowing between minds. It was a time when people were encouraged to study, learn and control the universe through knowledge and intelligence, not through faith in gods.

So I ask you again: If your attitude toward giving is related to the time and place in which you live, wouldn't it also be affected by the god you worship? Would you give to appease your god, to be in your god's favor? How much would this alter the amount you give? Most religions we practice today were founded more than a millennium ago—how much did the times during which they were formed affect what we give today?

There's clearly a correlation between the establishment of our religions and how we give today. We give partially because the religions we follow, those that have shaped us, were based on giving. They spread during times when trade was growing at exponential rates and people had to work with—and trust—strangers. They were built during times when more people were prospering.

The Golden Rule is "Treat others as you would like to be treated," and it's taught by all religions because the elders and the intellectuals saw how it benefited the people. Those who gave were those who prospered—spiritually, emotionally and financially. With the acceleration of trade and commerce, people were able to see firsthand the power of giving as it was put into practice. Those who saw it work were the ones who passed it on. Among them were Laozi, Moses, Jesus, Siddhartha, Socrates, Confucius and Muhammad. Religions aren't just about teaching the act of giving. They're about faith and belief—concepts linked to giving and success.

THE SCIENCE OF GIVING: DID GIVING EVOLVE?

In the previous section, we saw that religions were established to make the world a more harmonious place and that an important theme in the religious texts was the act of giving. Whether this was done to control people or to make them happier, or whether it was simply the general consensus, we can't really know.

One school of thought is that we gave long before religions were even formed, that giving is hard-wired in us. But another theory is that people didn't want to give—they were simply living in a society that promoted it. I want to say that our propensity to give is influenced biologically as much as it is religiously and socially. It has to be that way because there had to be a system of order among early hominids, ancient tribes and later societies to control and monitor the act of giving.

With help from the book *The Selfish Gene*, by Richard Dawkins, we can consider whether giving has in fact been a part of our makeup or whether it was taught to us by our societies and religions. Dawkins addresses the life of the human genome and how we pass our genes on from generation to generation and how the behaviors we adopt have come partly from our biological makeup. In terms of surviving, the idea of giving is actually counterintuitive. If you look at it from a biological point of view, it weakens us to give. As Dawkins says, "Selfish individuals prosper in the short term at the expense of altruists." If you give your food to your brother, you're taking nutrition away from your body and decreasing your chances of survival.

To this point, Dawkins says, "It often turns out on closer inspection that acts of apparent altruism are selfishness in disguise." Individual altruism is explained by the fundamental law he calls gene selfishness. To perpetuate the life of our genes, it's essential that we nurture and feed our children. We share half our genes with them, so we want those genes to be passed on to the next generation. But we also share half our genes with our siblings and our parents. Why do we give up more of our energy and food (today that equates to money) for our children than we do for our siblings and parents? It's because the larger our genetic carrying machines—our bodies—become, the more able they are to take care of themselves. We've evolved to a state in which we realize this, so we designate more of our energy and food to the genetic carrying machines that need it the most, our young.

To help explain the evolution to a state in which we choose to nurture the young rather than the old, Dawkins brings up an interesting phenomenon: When a woman ages, she loses energy but gains wisdom. So if she and her daughter had a baby at the same time, both babies would suffer. The mother's baby would suffer because she would be less capable of feeding and nurturing her baby. The daughter's baby would suffer because it would not receive the wisdom and maternal care that comes from a grandmother. The optimal result would be for the grandmother to forgo having babies and for the daughter to have more. We'll never know whether older females could control this urge to have more babies because nature has made that decision for them. Menopause puts a biological end to the grandmother's chances of bearing more children and allows her to be nurtured by more women.

Moreover, it was common for mothers to die in childbirth before the 20th century. So if you lost your mother in childbirth and were raised by your grandmother, you'd have been better fed and better able to survive in the world. If grandmothers also had babies, they too could die in childbirth, leaving the baby to be raised without maternal care. Menopause also prevents this from happening.

When it comes to basic survival, giving to our children is a non-reciprocal action. It's pleasurable to feed our young and to shelter them. We give in that way and we expect nothing in return.

Giving to Our Pets

Think about the relationship that people have with their pets. They buy them expensive cat and dog food. They keep them healthy by taking them to the veterinarian, to whom they often pay large sums of money. They wake up in the morning and feed their dogs and take them for walks even before feeding themselves.

Why do we love our pets so much? Because they show us love in return. Hundreds of thousands of years ago, dogs provided groups of hunters and gatherers not only with protection but also with help during the hunt. In villages throughout history, cats would eat the mice and rats, thereby alleviating the risk of disease. In turn, people fed them. During the Black Plague, it was mistakenly believed that cats were the carriers of the disease, and they were killed as a result. But it was actually the rats that were carrying the diseases, and by killing the cats that had been eating the rats, people actually amplified the rate of death caused by the plague.

Over time, those who kept dogs and cats as pets evolved to be safe from predators and disease while others died off. The dogs and cats stayed with people simply because they were fed by them. It's a simple symbiotic relationship—you scratch my back and I'll scratch yours.

There's a group of people called the Maasai in southern Kenya and northern Tanzania with a population of about a half-million people. They're semi-nomadic people who live under a communal land management system. [16] They've learned how to work with a species of bird called the honeyguide in order to find honey. The honeyguide has a scent for honey, and it directs the Maasai by changing its call when the Maasai get close to a hive. Once the Maasia obtain the honey from the hive, they leave a small honeycomb for the bird. But if they fail to reciprocate , the next time they ask for help in finding the honey, the bird leads them astray and the partnership disintegrates. [17]

The expectations are that we'll feed our animals and they'll help and protect us. This has evolved into a loving relationship in which our pets also keep us company and even lick our faces now and then. That's all we ask of them, and in turn we gladly spend billions of dollars a year on them. I'm a single person with no children, but I can only imagine that the feeling I get from taking care of my pets would be magnified a thousand times if I were caring for children. If only our expectations of reciprocation were as simple with people as our expectations of animals.

Gene selfishness has to do with the relationships in which "you scratch my back and I'll scratch yours." It's also based on the fact that I'm more likely to share food with relatives than with strangers. I share exactly half my genes with my sister and half with my parents. I also share a quarter of my genes with my grandparents and a quarter with my aunts and uncles. For my genes to survive into the next generation, it would be wise for me to look out not only for myself but also for my relatives. But why have giving and altruism expanded beyond families to encompass friends and strangers who share no genes? Dawkins explains:

> In a species whose members do not move around much, or whose members move in small groups, the chances may be good that any random individual you come across is fairly close kin to you. In this case the rule, be nice to any member of the species whom you meet, could have positive survival value, in this sense that a gene predisposing its possessors to obey the rule might become more numerous in the gene pool. This may be why altruistic behavior is so frequent in troops of monkeys and schools of whales.

And so, like monkeys and whales, we live in communities. We've come to give to strangers because they might be related to us. But we've evolved not only to give to other members of our community but also to give to those we've never met who live in distant places. This is a beautiful thing that humans have within them, the capacity to care for others.

"If a husband and wife have more children than they can feed, the state, which means the rest of the population, simply steps in and keeps the surplus children alive and healthy," Dawkins says. "The welfare state is perhaps the greatest altruistic system the animal kingdom has ever known. "

But where did it come from? Dawkins believes this behavior has been taught. "Genes that tend to make children that cheat have an advantage in the gene pool," he says. "If there is a human moral to be drawn, it is that we teach our children altruism, for we cannot expect it to be part of their biological nature. " If we're all cheaters, our societies will collapse.

In his imaginary society, there are two kinds of monkeys: cheaters and suckers (i.e., givers). As he describes it, "Suckers groom anybody who needs it, indiscriminately. Cheaters accept altruism from suckers, but they never groom anybody else, not even somebody who has previously groomed them."

If this society were to exist, the cheaters would always fare better than the suckers because they wouldn't have to use any energy to groom anybody else. They would receive grooming from the suckers, who would use their energy to groom without receiving grooming themselves unless it were from other suckers. In time, suckers would become extinct, along with the entire population. To save the population, a third party would come in called a grudger.

"Grudgers remember the cheats and don't groom them back," Dawkins says. Eventually, the cheaters would never be groomed unless they groomed the grudgers in return. In time, the cheaters would become extinct and a more altruistic population would take its place.

If all people are good, no one loses. But there are cheaters, people who don't give but only take from the society, and sometimes, if not caught, these people prosper. In our society, there are many cheaters, which we accept as a byproduct of this society. But we can't let the cheaters get out of control. Otherwise, the entire population will be overrun with them and nobody will prosper. In societies filled with cheaters, the population soon becomes extinct. But if we punish cheaters, we can alter their cheating behavior and realize a more functional society. Thus, giving to strangers and altruistic behavior have evolved because, besides rewarding those who give, we punish those who fail to do so.

Are we happy when we give because our parents, teachers and priests trained us to give? Or is it built into us biologically? Is giving inherent in our nature, or is it a result of nurture? Dawkins says that if you're a cheat and you cheat the givers, you'll have a short-term advantage. But in the long term, especially in our society, you'll be punished for being a cheat and rewarded with praise if you give.

We can assume that religions sprang up when the leaders of society had the epiphany that if we praise and reward altruistic behavior and punish cheating behavior, we'll have long-running, functional societies. This was due to the growing complexity of societies and the fact that people began to own responsibility for their destinies rather than to put all their faith in gods and the "divinity" of their rulers. The correlation between the rise in shipwrecks in the Mediterranean Sea around 500 BC and the creation of the Old Testament and the Axial Age illustrates how, in the course of human history, the propensity to give has increased as the resources and monies available to people have grown.

After the last ice age ended around 12,000 BC and the planet began to warm, farming and the domestication of animals became preferable to living as hunters and gatherers. By the 5th century BC, higher temperatures had led to an abundance of plants and animals to be harvested, eaten and traded by humans. [18] If trade was the cause of people's finding value in being more accommodating and more giving and the warming weather was the catalyst for trade, it could be argued that temperature is the reason we value giving today.

Still today, we as a species are, more so than we care to think, still controlled by our planet's weather and temperature. A study by a team from Columbia and Princeton universities and published in the Aug. 24h 2011, issue of *Nature* concluded that the weather phenomenon El Niño may have been the underlying cause of 21 percent of all civil conflicts from 1950 to 2004 and of almost 30 percent of conflicts in countries where El Niño has a high impact. [19] Occurring every five years, El Niño is related to the temperature changes in the Pacific Ocean and can create extreme weather such as floods and droughts. It has such profound effects on agriculture that it can lead to starvation, a prospect that can spark aggression among people and even start civil wars.

Is the Earth getting hotter? Clearly, it is. Are we going to experience more El Niño cycles? Possibly. So how does this impact the amount we give? What if the Earth got hotter or colder? Would we be less likely to give? According to the Columbia-Princeton study, yes, we'd be less likely to give and live harmoniously and more likely to be violent. So it stands to reason that when our governments know an El Niño is coming, practices should be put into place that enhance giving and its benefits and minimize the risk of conflict. If we're going to be more hostile to one another as the Earth gets hotter, let's understand that this hostility will only diminish our productivity and well being. Let's remember that giving helps to harmonize society. Of course, this is easier said than done. When someone has a "mob mentality," he doesn't recall the lessons he's learned about being a lawful citizen. Instead, he gets swept up in the movement. The same holds true when the weather changes, and it's up to our leaders to remain levelheaded during these moments and to break the spell we're under.

In times when resources, food, shelter and opportunity are scarce, people tend to stop giving and start hoarding. This makes intuitive sense because giving would be detrimental to our own survival. But what happens is that people begin to turn on one another. They don't benefit from the symbiosis of sharing, and eventually they turn on their leaders and rulers. To avoid this calamity, we need to have constant access to food, never engage in war and always have enough to share with each other. Unfortunately, that's impossible, but if we recognize that the fall of our social traditions is caused by the scarcity around us, we can also recognize that if we don't lose our heads and we continue to share and give, we'll solve whatever problems arise.

To summarize: We can make the connection that religions were established as the number of boats on the Mediterranean Sea reached a peak between 500 BC and 400 BC. Trade and wide-ranging relationships grew during this time as well. The more boats that were crossing from port to port, the more people were rubbing elbows with each other.

I am suggesting that, along with trade and relationships, giving increased too. We know that religions were based on giving. We can assume that people understood both the benefit and the detriment of taking. This was illustrated by Dawkins' example of the monkeys. The societies that lasted had grudgers who forced the act of giving to increase and the act of taking to decrease. Religious leaders passed on the wisdom of giving in their times, and to this day, the impact of their works has been a part of the zeitgeist.

Religion plays a large role in our cultures and in our actions. From a biological point of view, this is unwise, but in the short term, giving has become valued in all societies. Religions and their texts are like an elder who's gathering the tribe to teach the youths the traditions and practices that will serve them well. With the help of religions and elders such as Moses, Buddha, Confucius, Jesus and Muhammad who tell us what is right and what helps society to prevail, we have come to learn that giving is good and that we're rewarded for practicing it.

WHO TO GIVE TO?

When we give, we trust someone to give back to us. But with that comes vulnerability. We become open to being taken advantage of, and by giving we risk losing our energy, money or time without reciprocation. In Dawkins' scenario of the suckers, cheaters and grudgers, it would make sense to give to the suckers or the grudgers but not to give to the cheaters. The problem is that you don't know who's a sucker, a cheater or a grudger until you get to know them or until you pick ticks off of their backs.

Ideally, we want to give to our friends and family. We want to give our time to our work. We want to give to ourselves by exercising and learning. But if we focus only on our friends, our family and ourselves, we fail to benefit from what the rest of the world has to offer. If we don't try to give to strangers or new acquaintances and we don't test their reciprocation and generosity, we miss the opportunity to benefit from them.

We need to be wise grudgers. Did someone give back to you? Did he give back but not what you thought he should have? To know if strangers are truly worthy of giving, we have to extend the olive branch. If they give back, they are; if they don't, we may have to pull back the reins.

BUSINESS AND GIVING

As grudgers and knowing how to spot a taker and a cheat our feelings to corporations are especially suspicious. In big business and small, it's important to have good communication. Generally speaking, the more you give, the more people will seek you out. This applies whether you're bringing cookies to share with your co-workers, sharing knowledge with them or simply giving a pat on the back to a subordinate. And the more people seek you out, the more communicating you're likely to do, thus enhancing the flow of information and the amount of business that gets shared and accomplished with and through you. How many times have you heard of a business that went awry because the boss was unapproachable and didn't know what was going on with his staff?

When it comes to business, giving is vital. People today look at businesses as living, breathing entities with a face and a soul. In a single interaction, a business makes an impression on a person. Whether it's a telephone conversation or an in-store experience, a customer judges a business every time he interacts with it. To improve the feelings our consumers have for us, we need to give to them.

If I'm in the market for a pair of jeans and Company A will sell them to me for $50 and not give me anything else while Company B will realize a profit by selling them to me for $100 but also gives me something like points toward future purchases, I'm more likely to buy from Company B. Many companies do this as a means of attaining customer loyalty.

Shoppers Drug Mart® is the largest drugstore chain in Canada. With every purchase you make, you're awarded points. When you've accumulated enough points, you receive free products. This discourages you from buying shampoo, pharmaceuticals or toilet paper from another store. By giving to you and making you feel foolish if you shop elsewhere, Shoppers Drug Mart retains you as a loyal customer.

It's important for companies not to forget about the act of giving and its benefits. As we've seen, giving is a long-term process that doesn't always pay dividends immediately, but if you ask any company CEO or sales representative about the benefits of the process, he'll tell you it's better to retain a customer than to find a new one. It's also less expensive. So while giving helps retain long-term customers, it also cuts costs for the business as a whole.

Another good way to use giving as a business tool is to give to charities or nonprofit organizations. This is known as "cause marketing." Not only will it get you noticed, but you'll also help society in the process.

For every pair of shoes it sells, the footwear company Toms® gives a pair of shoes to a needy child who lives in a poor area of America or in a developing country such as Zimbabwe. Toms® is doing a great thing for society *and* capitalizing on the act of giving. It doesn't have to spend money on advertising, because it gets the consumer's attention from the public relations built into its business model. When you wear a pair of Toms® shoes, you're supporting something much bigger than yourself, and that can only mean good word of mouth.

When someone sees that your company gives to a charity, you catch his attention. Consider the following scenario: Joan is looking for a jar of pickles in a grocery store. She notices that there's a variety of brands and flavors to choose from. She also notices that for every jar of Yummy Pickles that's purchased, the Yummy Company gives a dollar to a charity. Which brand of pickles do you think she's most likely to buy?

It's been determined that people respond to organizations that work with charities that help the environment or give back to the community in some way. Many businesses have pounced on this idea and benefited greatly from it. Those that haven't have often seen their competitors steal their share of the market. As we have seen, it's wired in us to give; it helped our societies to flourish and our communities to be more harmonious. Subconsciously, we've always known this, and packaging our products in a way that lets the consumer know we help society makes them more likely to buy our products.

At the same time, be careful of hypocrisy. Why are you giving? Why are you sponsoring that charity? If you don't have a direct answer other than that you want to look good or to be seen as charitable, people will sniff you out as a fraud.

When KFC® was doing a promotion for breast-cancer research, it donated 50 cents to the cause for every bucket of chicken sold. This enraged consumers. Fifteen thousand e-mails arrived at the head office asking how the company had the audacity to sponsor something like a cure for breast cancer when studies have shown that KFC sells food that's bad for our health. Like many other companies, KFC® was clearly "milking the disease."

In the television series Mad Men, protagonist Don Draper epitomizes the concept of marketing. He's good looking, has a beautiful wife and two beautiful children, a boy and a girl. He dresses nicely and perpetuates the illusion that he's the perfect human being. This is what businesses attempt to do as well. Whether through radio, television, the Internet or via public relations, their ad campaigns attempt to create the illusion that they're great companies that sell great products that will make you skinnier, better looking and happier. However, the truth is that Don Draper is a fraud. He has a terrible marriage. His past life connects him to nobody. He drinks heavily. And he takes credit for work he doesn't do. He's a fraud. The same may hold true for any number of businesses.

As we get to know Don better and as we get to know those companies better, we see that in this illusion lies weakness. In this illusion, there lie unhappy employees. In this illusion, there lie managers who care only about bonuses and not about the trees in the forests that they order to be cut down in the process.

Over time, false marketing begins to smell. In the eyes of the general public, your message comes to sound contradictory. Just like with Don, we smell a fake. This is why it's so important to be real. Don't give faultily. It's better not to give at all than it is to give for ugly ulterior motives like recognition and profits. You have to practice what you preach or your image will suffer.

Make sure you're more like Toms® than KFC®. Have a reason for associating yourself with a given charity, and make sure the connection is a believable one. Maybe you could arrange for the marketing coordinator to survey the employees in your workplace and determine a cause they'd like to fight for. That way, you'll have a more compelling reason for giving to a cause than that your product matches the colors in the charity's logo.

Customer complaints represent another giving opportunity for businesses. In an episode of the television series The Simpsons, young Lisa Simpson tries to encourage her father, Homer, by saying that the Chinese use the same word for crisis as they do for opportunity. Homer then says, "Ah, crisi-tunity!" We should remember this concept and look at a complaint as an opportunity to secure a new customer. Usually, people who are calling in with a complaint are the most outspoken. A negative encounter with your customer service department can be disastrous for your company. If the customer is asking for something, give it to him. If you don't, or if you fail to meet his expectations, he'll tell his friends, and then their friends will tell their friends. However, if you give them something, if you go above and beyond the call of duty, they'll begin to like you. Not only will they keep your company in mind the next time they're shopping, but they might even go out of their way to buy something of yours. By giving to them, you can foster a harmonious relationship.

Many companies' customer-service departments offer $20 gift cards, which is a wise practice. When you go to a store like Lululemon® or Guess®, your purchases are rarely just $20. In fact, the average purchase at those stores is probably in the hundreds of dollars. So by issuing gift cards or coupons that have low dollar amounts, these companies entice you into entering their stores and spending much more than $20—another example of giving being used as an effective marketing tool.

You might be surprised to know that companies save money when they employ more people in their customer service departments. But then, it makes perfect sense. The more people you employ to receive calls from customers, the more you'll see the early signs of a defective product and the fewer trucks you'll have to dispatch later in order to fix broken products.

One of the best marketing tools for consumer goods is the practice of giving away samples. Many people would never try your product unless you gave them free samples. Just like advertising on radio or television, giving away samples lets the consumer know about your product, and your rate of sales will rise as a result. In the marketing community, this is called *seeding* a product. Companies essentially plant seeds by issuing you free products, and those seeds grow and become actual purchases.

One of the most successful toys to hit the market in the past few years are Zhu Zhu pets, battery-operated pets that move around at their own discretion. They became so popular after the marketing team handed them out for free to millions of Americans at baseball games. Clearly, the seeding worked. Once they owned one, kids wanted to collect the whole assortment.

Another good marketing ploy is to give away pens, pads of paper, or any other small items that have your company's name written on them. I once received a pair of nail clippers from the Cathay Pacific® airline and have owned them for years, so I've come to associate durability and reliability with that airline. Every time I use them, I think of that company. In the airline business, this is one of the most important criteria for customers. Promotional items are a great way for customers not only to keep your company in the forefront of their mind but also to associate you with that item. Keep in mind that if you aren't careful, this can backfire. If you skimp on cost and put your name on a cheap promotional item, you might actually associate yourself with tackiness.

A new form of seeding products for long-term profit has emerged in the world of software applications. Many apps are given away for free, but once consumers become hooked on them, they discover that they can obtain additional features for them if they pay an extra $1, $5 or sometimes $20. Ultimately, the free trial helps to coax customers into making future purchases. Many games and service apps have made a lot of money this way.

Businesses can also give away information. It's almost as common for businesses to have Twitter and Facebook accounts and websites as it is for them to have telephone numbers, and they can use them to build confidence in their products. Dr. Oz's website RealAge,™ for example, provides information about ways to stay fit and healthy. When people receive his weekly newsletter by e-mail, Dr. Oz is in the forefront of their minds, and they tune in later to watch him on television. When he publishes a book, they're likely to buy it. Because he's using other mediums to gain our trust and confidence, we gladly pay for his next piece of work.

In the 1950s, the only way a company could announce its good deeds was by word of mouth, using newspapers and radio. It was difficult to reach a critical mass of people, to say the least. Today we can also use the Internet to broadcast our good deeds.

So, for example, if a stroller company arranged for a group of employees to give away strollers to young families in a random neighborhood, they could take pictures of the smiling mothers who received those products and then post them on the company website or send them to a local news station. The good deed, which affected a small neighborhood of young mothers, is then publicized and broadcast to a much wider audience.

This is known as guerrilla marketing, and the objective is to create a unique, engaging and thought-provoking concept in order to generate buzz. When we do a good deed, we can package it and make it viral for all the world to see. This creates positive associations with our company.

Giving Inside Your Organization

In the national bestseller *The Breakthrough Company*, author Keith McFarland says, "Involving people in strategy is just one of the things business can do to drive commitment. Maybe the best way to get the right people on the bus is to create a bus worth riding on in the first place." He uses the term *clock builders* to describe people who build companies with ideologies and principles that can be passed on to the next generation of managers and leaders.

In October 2011, Steve Jobs, renowned CEO of Apple Inc., died of pancreatic cancer. Many people outside the company worried about the future of Apple without him. After all, since 1996, he'd taken the company from $2 billion to $330 billion in sales. Will the company carry on at this rate for the next five to ten years? If it has established an ideology and a set of values that can keep it going, there's every reason to believe it will. (As I write this, Apple is still kicking ass.)

In the book *Built To Last*, author Jim Collins says the visionary companies that last the longest are those whose founders establish an ideology that can stand the test of time. Either they have a clear ideology that's real and that people can believe in, or they have goals that stimulate progress and keep people excited. If current management hews to the founders' ideology and firmly believe in it, the company will fare well. But for this to happen, the founders have to embrace the fact that they won't manage the company forever and that they need to set up a dogma on which the future of the company can run.

Let's look at a couple of examples. The goal of Procter and Gamble is to improve the lives of everyday families, and the goal of the Wal-Mart corporation is to offer the lowest prices. These companies have been doing business for many years because the founders knew that, for their companies to last, they would need to give their future leaders principles that could stand the test of time and keep them excited.

McFarland points out in his book that the best companies are the ones whose leaders have surrounded themselves with good people in order to help them learn and navigate through difficult times—and vice versa. These leaders understand that they don't know everything, so they seek help from a core support system. The smartest man is the one who knows that he knows nothing, Beware the man who thinks he knows everything.

Even the most cherished musical group of all time, The Beatles, needed support to reach the top. It was with the help of manager Brian Epstein and producer George Martin that they influenced an entire generation and changed the way we look at music. Without that help, they may not have had the impact they did.

In every Oscar speech, someone says "thank you" to someone else for his or her support and positive words. Most people who become successful do so with the support and positivity of others.

Relationships and Partnering

As an entrepreneur, or anything else for that matter, you need to find fellow givers. When you do, continue giving to them. If they happen to be your website designers, for example, pay them early. If they're your sales representatives, give them excellent commission rates. If they're your best employees, offer them extended vacations. If you continue to give to them, they will continue to give back to you. The best companies not only have long-lasting ideologies and a solid support system, but they're also good at giving to their employees.

Whole Foods Market® is the world's largest retailer of natural and organic foods. Its staff members aren't known as "staff"—they're known as "the owners" and are given shares in the company. The idea is that this encourages them to consider themselves crucial to the company's success as a whole (excuse the pun). Any employer being accoladed for his company's success will humbly tell you that the people who work for him are better than he is. It's paramount to keep these people.

Simply put, if you teach and trust your best employees, they'll repay you. If you're worried that they'll leave you and you decide not to teach them or help them grow, you'll fulfill the prophecy of their imminent departure. To keep them, you have to be giving to them, not only by showering them with appreciation but also by giving them a higher purpose. These people are smart, so they need to have a good reason to show up for work. Making sure they know they're doing something great is vital. Sit down with your staff members and discuss incentives and goals with them. One-third of our lives is spent working, so ensure that your team is happy to be working together and sharing a common goal. Giving employees compliments is underrated. Even something as simple as "You're dealing really well" or "Nice work on the case" can boost their motivation significantly.

NETWORKING

Whether you're an entrepreneur, a manager or an employee, networking is key to success. I've talked about people who give to strangers and how they run the risk of not being reciprocated, but you can also choose not to give to strangers. In that case, though, you run the risk of missing the opportunity of *being* reciprocated and making a new friend.

Those who choose to give are those who are good at networking. They often give before they even know if the person is a giver or a cheater. Whether they give a compliment to a fellow classmate they're meeting for the first time or they buy a competitor a drink at a bar, the best networkers are the first to introduce themselves. They never fail to miss these opportunities because they see them for what they are: chances to make new friends and establish mutually beneficial relationships. They know that the more circles they travel in, the better off they'll be. They'll be privy to more information, they'll build the trust of others and they'll gain from their wisdom and knowledge. The most successful people are those who know the right people.

But who are the right people?

If you want to find the winning lottery ticket, you're more likely to find it by buying more tickets. The same holds true for people—you're more likely to find the right person by meeting more people. That's why it's been found that those who network are the most successful.

Let's examine the professional lives of two extroverts, Dale and Marissa. Dale is head of the finance department. He receives the trust and respect of everyone in the department, but he never speaks to the people who work in the other departments. Dale will do well in his career, but he won't benefit from the networking that Marissa does.

Marissa works in the sales department. Every morning, she speaks to Laura in the human resources department, and once a week she eats lunch with Kevin in the finance department. She keeps abreast of what's going on in the whole office, not just in her own department. As a result, she'll probably gain the respect and trust of the most important person in the organization, the boss. When it comes to networking, the goal should be to listen to everyone and try to understand everything.

The opportunities for meeting new people are endless, and networking is thus a never-ending job.

NEGOTIATION

Whenever you're in negotiations with someone, it's important to leave an impression as a fair and smart person. That's why it's wise to reach a just agreement even if it's an agreement that benefits the other side more than it benefits yours. If you think the deal is fair, there's a chance that the other side will believe they were cheated and that you benefited more than they did. They won't want to deal with you in the future and you'll have lost a customer, a client or a supplier. So if you give a little more to the other side, you're more likely to do business with him in the future and you'll realize profits for years to come. If you give today, you invest in your future. A city builder needs to ensure that all his bridges are stable and grounded, and the same holds true in business. We're all islands, and we have to make sure all our bridges—our relationships—are strong.

Many people choose not to give today out of fear that if they will never do business with a person or company in the future, their altruism will go unrewarded. They think that in the grand scheme of things, the act of giving will cost them. But givers are different. They have faith that they'll do business with a company again in the future, so their harmonious approach is rewarded down the road in the form of goodwill and positive word of mouth. Just like with negotiation, if you want to be in the sales game for long, you have to be a partner whom the other side views as fair, or even beneficial to them.

In the toy business, there are a handful of small players, but only Hasbro and Mattel realize more than $5 billion in sales a year. One reason these two companies have been so successful for so long is that they have the capability of accepting payment back from retailers long after their products have been sold to the consumer. Their terms are 90 to 120 days—the number of days retailers have to pay for their goods once they're shipped. The other players in the toy game require the payment sooner.

If you run a distribution chain of stores such as Toys "R" Us or Target, who would you want to buy toys from, the company that needs to be paid before the items are sold in your store or the company that can wait for payment until much later? If you want to stay in the game, you have to give something, even if it's only terms that benefit your customers.

When you cut corners, people know and they won't use your products again. Of course, they'll have to pay a higher price for items of a higher quality, but they're more willing to do that than you think. With Apple Inc., people pay a premium for the assurance that what they get is the top-of-the-line product on the market. They pay for more than a computer—they pay for a guarantee their computer will work. If you give people what they want, they'll flock to buy your products or services. Ralph Waldo Emerson famously said, "Build a better mousetrap and the world will beat a path to your door."

Here are some other ways you can give:

- Value: Offer good margins and a good price.
- Guaranteed sale: Be willing to take back your goods if they don't sell. Note: This is risky, as you can become stuck with obsolete inventory.
- Innovation: Product is king. Be as innovative as you can.
- Professionalism: On-time delivery eases retailers' stress and anxiety about getting product in time for the selling period.
- Advertising: I studied marketing in school and was always doubtful of people's likelihood of buying something just because it was advertised. I thought we were more immune to the hypnotism of advertising. I was wrong. When you run a commercial on TV or engage in PR activities like

giving away samples, people are that much more likely to buy your product.

- Good packaging: Packaging is an important aspect of any product. Why do you buy the wine that's from the same country and has the same price tag as the wine beside it? Sometimes the answer is purely the aesthetics of the packaging.

THE ECONOMICS OF GIVING

Giving is reciprocal. If you give, you'll get back.

A few months ago, I was in a feng shui shop and I asked the shopkeeper what he thought about giving and how it related to feng shui. He looked at me and said very seriously, "People don't realize that if you give an inch, you get a yard." To those who give, the universe responds tenfold. Look at giving as a bank or a vault—the more you deposit into the vault, the more interest you earn on your gift. Wouldn't you rather earn interest on your money than leave it sitting under your mattress collecting dust?

You can also compare giving to gardening. You need to water your plants if you want to grow beautiful zucchinis, luscious eggplants, juicy raspberries and ripe tomatoes. If you stop watering the plants, they'll wither away and die. When people ask, "What have you done for me lately?" they're simply telling you that you haven't watered your relationship in a while.

You need to give continuously if you want to reap the rewards of giving.

And the relationships that require the most "water" often bring the highest rewards. Giving to the needy carries a higher reward than giving when there's little risk that you won't be reciprocated. When we give to those who need it the most, sometimes we risk our lives. Think of the Holocaust or helping slaves. During the Holocaust, a few Christians hid Jews in their barns or their basements in order to protect their lives. If they'd been caught, those Christians would have been imprisoned or killed. You often hear about Holocaust survivors or their offspring retuning to the homes of those Christians to thank them. They'll never forget the good deeds and altruism of these people. They'll be forever grateful.

From the 1600s to the 1860s, many people helped to free African-American slaves. Like the Jews, these people will never forget the help they received in the face of death or imprisonment. You'll always have two friends at opposite ends of the wheel of fate, one up and the other down. It's important to give to both of them. The friend who's up is a good person to give to because he has the means to give back to you, but it's more important to give to the friend who's down because he'll never forget the kindness you showed him when he needed it the most.

I'm involved in the toy business, where I hope to remain for many years to come. I'll never forget those who welcomed me into the industry and those who treated me like a child. When you start a new job, let alone one in which your father has left his own mark, there's a certain degree of stress and anxiety that accompanies it. Those people who welcomed me and helped to ease my anxiety will always hold a special place in my heart. And I hope my reciprocation to these people will meet or exceed their expectations. Whether they understood that, by embracing me, they would lead me to want to repay them, I don't know when, but I'll give back to them in spades, whether through loyalty, goodwill, partnerships or referrals.

Do people like giving money to each other? That depends on whom they're giving it to. Are you giving to a homeless person? If so, you know your money will never be returned. Are you giving to a brother or sister or to your mother and father? If so, you often expect the money to come back. If it doesn't, you'll be mortally disappointed and may never speak to your relatives again.

When you give $10 to a homeless person, he'll be grateful, but if you give him $100, he'll never forget it. The rewards of giving are compounded. If you continue to give to people in good times (financially or emotionally), they'll be there for you when you experience bad times. As we saw with the example of the vault, giving is almost like buying insurance or a GIC. It's about safety. Most people will visit a friend in the hospital if he's injured, or they'll offer their condolences if a co-worker's relative passes away. But if they invite you to their home to attend a party that you know not many people will attend, your friend will never forget you. If you ever need them, they will be there for you in some way.

Just like with the act of investing, the act of giving is long-term. We might think we should be rewarded the very day after we throw that huge party or the very moment we walk out of a building where we donated a large amount of money to charity, but giving is much more long-term than that. A good example is the concept of making a point to wish someone a happy birthday. It sticks with people. They don't forget you or what you did for them. It's imperative to look at giving in that way.

There's a calendar in my mother's office on which she has marked all her friends' birthdays. On each of these days, she sends a birthday card and then calls or e-mails them. When her own birthday rolls around, the countertop in our kitchen is filled with birthday cards. There's no doubt that they make her feel appreciated and loved. These cards are her plants. Because she watered her friends with birthday wishes, they gave her birthday wishes in return.

Wishing someone a happy birthday is a cultural custom we've developed to remind people we care about them. Other norms, such as bringing a bouquet of flowers when we're invited to someone's home, have also been established over time. There was a *Seinfeld* episode where Jerry, Elaine, Kramer and George are invited to a friend's home and Elaine suggests they stop on the way to get a bottle of wine. George says that he doesn't drink wine and that they should bring Coke instead and, for that matter, why do they have to bring anything at all? Elaine snarls at him, "Because we are adults." Like

George, it seems that many people don't understand that when they're invited to the home of a friend, they should bring something. It can be something as small as a bag of potato chips or something as extravagant as a crystal vase. But many people haven't been taught this common courtesy even though it would benefit them. If no one else brings something, you'll be the outlier and you'll be rewarded greatly for it. By the same token, if everyone gives a little something and you bring something more valuable, you'll be the one who stands out. But that isn't much of a problem today—most people don't bring anything when they visit a friend. So by simply bringing a bag of potato chips, you'll be labeled a giver, and eventually you'll benefit from your gracious acts of kindness.

Another important aspect of giving is the thought that occurs in someone's mind after he buys someone a gift. When my sister and her boyfriend moved into their new home, I gave them a barbecue as a housewarming gift. I'd made plans to go out to dinner with a friend that week, so immediately after I made the purchase, I realized that if I wanted to give to others, treat myself and still maintain my financial budget, I had to work harder. I realized that I had to earn more in order to justify spending more, something those who often give have realized, too.

This makes sense. If we all gave a little more, we'd have to work harder in order to justify it. Economists realize this, and that's why they advise the government and the banks to provide incentives for people to spend more money. There's no doubt that Christmas gift-giving was created specifically for this purpose. So why doesn't everyone give in order to spur the economy? The answer is that they think they can't afford to. That's the difference between those who are successful and those who aren't, the faith that they'll always be able to make money.

David Ricardo was an English political economist. In 1817 he wrote a book called *On the Principles of Political Economy and Taxation.* In it he describes the well-known theory of comparative advantage whereby two societies trade with one another and end up better off because of it. From a macroeconomic standpoint, David Ricardo's comparative advantage illustrates how giving can benefit societies and those who trade with one another. If one country makes the best peanut butter and another country makes the best jelly, they both benefit if they decide to trade with one another. If they both focus on the quality of their own product and trade with one another, they can have the best of everything. Sometimes we hear arguments against globalization and the outsourcing of jobs, but the truth is that we live in a globalized world now, and with globalization we all benefit from one another. As nations we understand this, but as individuals we're reluctant to acknowledge it.

We can apply Ricardo's comparative advantage to ourselves as individuals, too. In every time period, there have been people who have had more than others. If we could forget about one another's net worth and the number of possessions that each of us has, we'd all be better off. Wealthy people will be better off because they won't have poor people demanding higher rates of taxation or goods from them. Poor people will be better off because they'll be treated fairly. They'll be allowed to enjoy not only the benefits of their input into the economy but everyone else's efforts as well. The fewer freeloaders there are in the world, the more benefits the rest of us can enjoy and the better the world becomes. But this begins with each individual.

When we talk about the economics of giving, we must discuss the government and the role it plays in increasing the likelihood that its people will give to one another, work hard and appreciate and revere fairness and trust. For example, the Obama administration allows workers to receive up to 99 weeks of unemployment benefits, but this encourages them to remain unemployed for longer periods of time. The average unemployed worker collects benefits for 40 weeks, and this promotes taking. Even though it puts money into their hands, which spurs the economy in the short term, it ultimately does a disservice to the economy. The government must establish programs that create jobs, because the longer you're out of the workforce, the harder it is to return. Too many people out of the workforce take from the government and others, and this leads to a weak economy.

As complex civilizations have developed, the idea that everyone can benefit from giving and sharing has blossomed. In his book *The Rational Optimist*, Matt Ridley points out that most of the things in your life are the works of others. Your car, television, shower stall, food, books, bedding, telephone, chairs, pens, hats and towels have all been thought of, created, built, maintained and, in some cases, marketed by other people. Each of us either chooses to do a job in society or free-rides the system designed hundreds of years ago by the division of labor. Our capitalist society has created a world in which one person does one thing and another person does another. We all benefit from each other's work and feel the pain from one another's unemployment.

Both David Ricardo and Adam Smith, the Scottish pioneer of political economy, would be impressed with the current state of capitalism, even though some of us think we're doomed. In the late 1700s, Adam Smith wrote that if markets are big, everyone can produce what they can make the cheapest and the best, and then when they sell those things, they can use the profits to buy whatever else they need. That would make everyone wealthier than if they tried to make everything for themselves. He wrote that we should become good at something so we can give it away and, in return, get goods that we *aren't* good at making. In capitalism and a free market, people are able to work as hard as they want and take responsibility for their actions, efforts and incomes.

COMMON CHARACTERISTICS OF THE SUCCESSFUL

Successful people have faith. They have faith in themselves, in other people and in the universe. They truly believe that if they do something good, they'll be repaid for it in some way. They understand patience. If they give to a friend, a stranger, or even to themselves, they understand that the results of their good deed won't necessarily be seen today or even tomorrow. But they will see them someday.

Whenever you wonder if the efforts you put into a long-term project are worth it, just know that they are. You'll never really be able to quantify it, but you'll be paid back at some point. Even if you worked on something for a long time and it didn't materialize the way you thought it would, you still learned a lot and polished some skills. Don't quit because you failed once.

European and Chinese businessmen and policymakers often wonder why America creates the Mark Zuckerbergs and the Steve Jobses of the world. The answer lies in Americans' acceptance that failure is part of the path that leads to success. Apple Inc. released many products that were financial flops, but Jobs and his team knew they needed to fail in order to learn and achieve success. The best companies understand that innovation comes from errors and mistakes. The reason that innovation isn't rampant in other places is that they don't share this philosophy. They don't believe failures are a good thing. Those who have faith they will succeed dust themselves off and continue inventing after a failure. These are the people who will create the next Facebook, Google or Ipod.

It's not about what happens to you. Nor is it about how others receive your thoughts, ideas or inventions. It's about how you react to the successes and failures in life. During his career, Babe Ruth held the record for committing the most strikeouts. But he also hit the most home runs in his time. Winston Churchill said, "Success consists of going from failure to failure without loss of enthusiasm."

The thing about fear of failure is that it's inaccurate. When you focus so much thought on the worst, you're not thinking about reality; being the victim of a serious automobile accident or losing everything you own will never happen to 99 percent of us. Faith, however, is accurate. The positive thoughts we have when we think about the future can, in fact, come true, and they can help us construct our world for the better. You should never fear that your efforts won't materialize. Just know that if you have faith, they will.

In Napoleon Hill's book *Think and Grow Rich*, from the 1930s, he said, "Faith and fear make poor bedfellows. Where one is found the other cannot exist." The book is based on the universal law of attraction, which developed from the New Thought philosophy of the 1890s and holds that what we focus on develops into our reality. [20] The concept has been made newly popular by the book and movie *The Secret*, which suggests that you can attain anything you want simply by asking the universe for it. It requires that you be specific in what you ask for, believe you'll receive it and be accepting of it once it arrives. The last requirement is the most difficult for some of us. Receiving what we asked for can be problematic because we may believe we're undeserving of wealth or joy or a family. Some of us believe that if good things happen to us, bad things are sure to come in like a storm and take them away. We need to understand that good things can happen to us without repercussion. Everything in our life can be good all at the same time. If you're a spiritual person, I suggest you make the time to watch *The Secret*.

Those who overcome fear become successful. They tell themselves that they will be safe, that they will have abundance and that they will be loved. They tell themselves that giving is no cost to them; rather, it's an opportunity to see future rewards. On the other hand, takers see the world in a darker light. They think that if they give to a friend or a stranger or to a son or a daughter, they're losing something in the act. We need to appreciate that they don't understand the benefits of giving. Maybe they were raised not to give by parents who believed they hadn't received fair reciprocation from others or the universe. Maybe their parents were raised during the Great Depression and *their* parents worked hard only to receive pennies at the end of the day. And when they saw that their efforts amounted to so little, they became angry and turned a cold shoulder to the world, raising takers of their own. Or maybe they experienced unrequited love in their teenage years, all their acts of giving seeming to lead to heartbreak and rejection. So giving—to anything and anyone—is distasteful to them.

These people lack an understanding of the power of giving. They haven't overcome their fears about giving and whether it will be returned to them. They see giving as a loss. They don't have faith that giving will repay them. These people aren't necessarily takers—they're simply non-givers. Unlike successful givers, they don't see that giving requires us to think long-term, that it will bring us benefits and reciprocation later. They've lost patience and have given up on giving because they didn't see immediate benefits.

Givers know that there's a lag between their altruistic acts and their rewards. Sometimes a belief in superstition and the idea of karma help them cope with that lag. If you wake up every morning and tap your nose three times for good luck, that's your "thing." As John Lennon once said, "Whatever gets you through your life, it's all right." If one day you forget to do your thing, no one in the universe is going to care, because it doesn't affect them. But it does affect you. That's the idea behind superstition. If it works for you, if it puts an extra kick in your step and helps you to think positively, then do it. Whether giving actually gives you karma or not can never be determined tangibly, but if you have faith that it will, then continue giving. As we've seen, there are many benefits to giving, and if you believe it will provide you with that extra advantage in life—if it's your thing—do it for that reason, too.

My father has been in the toy business for 25 years. After watching him my whole life, I now work alongside him. Like many toy businessmen, he often travels to Hong Kong. He once told me he gave money every day to a homeless woman there who sat just outside the building where he worked. Dropping a few coins or Hong Kong dollars into her cup was a ritual that gave him a boost. Whether it actually improved his performance is impossible to measure, but it didn't' hurt it. Once he'd dropped a coin into the cup, besides feeling good about it, he believed good things were bound to happen to him that day.

Giving can give us positive karma, but to benefit from it, we have to have faith in it. There's no way to prove this to be true, but it's a secret the successful share. When we give, we get back tenfold.

Adam Sandler, Howard Stern and the fictional Vince Chase from *Entourage* understand the concept of giving. These men are chronic givers. Not only do they entertain people, but they're forever employing their closest friends. They need a support system of people who will love them for who they are, regardless of their celebrity status—and that's more important than getting back exactly what they give. What Stern, Sandler and Chase get for helping their friends isn't monetary and tangible but rather emotional and intangible. They give to their circle of friends because, in return, they receive loyalty and goodwill. These men trust that what they give will be returned to them. The successful give constantly. It's a part of their motivation to get up in the morning and earn money so that they can not only afford luxuries but continue giving.

We need to have faith that our giving is going to come back to us. Successful givers have this faith, not only about giving but also about business, sports, war and even life itself. The successful giver believes that he'll succeed even when there is little evidence to support that belief.

Many of us approach both sports and business like we approach war. We often use terms like *attack, battle, defeat, succeed* and *overcome*. Like in wars, the activities we partake in throughout our lives have a higher degree of success if we look at them in a positive and optimistic light. When we have faith, it allows us mental support to push that extra iota. We enjoy watching sports because a sport is like a war, not in the sense of life and death but because the same principles apply to the winners who persevere and beat the odds. They work as a team. They think positively and heroes emerge.

Dr. Martin Seligman, a mental-health expert and creator of the first master's program in the world to offer in-depth study of the science of well-being, created the term *learned optimism* to describe the mentality that good things are permanent and bad things are temporary. In 1985, Seligman and his team of researchers read all the sports pages in the hometown papers of each National League baseball team—about 15,000 pages of sports reporting. They discovered that the way the coach and the players phrased their reactions to their most recent win or loss dictated their level of success in the future. If they lost and believed it was just one bad game, they'd be able to bounce back faster and win the next game. Additionally, if they won and said something indicating permanence like "We're the best team—we always win under pressure," they'd cement their success, making winning a part of the team psyche. [21]

In 2011, a squirrel ran onto the field during a playoff game in St. Louis between the Cardinals and the Philadelphia Phillies, and from then on Cardinals fans wore squirrel memorabilia. The Cardinals went on to defeat the heavily favored Phillies, and in the World Series they came back in the bottom of both the ninth and tenth innings of Game 6 to force a seventh game against the Texas Rangers. And guess who won Game 7? The Cardinals clearly believed destiny was with them, and it truly was. When you believe something is destined to be, you become unstoppable.

In sports and everything else, the successful have faith. When you give, you need to have faith that your giving will come back. If you don't, you won't give and reap the rewards. Faith comes in different forms, be it a superstition regarding cats or squirrels running across dugouts or a belief in destiny. Whatever it is, the success you believe in will eventually become reality. Granted, the time that separates belief and reality can be hard to endure, but superstition, religion and a belief in karma can be effective coping mechanisms—whatever works.

Giving Anonymously

I told my grandmother's best friend that I was writing this book, and she said she found the topic of giving very interesting and asked if I was I going to mention anything about anonymity. She told me that when she'd stayed in a hospital for months to be with her ailing husband, there were photos on a wall of the many wealthy people who'd donated to the hospital and a list of how much or what they'd donated. "I wondered why these people had given to the hospital and then wanted recognition for it", she said. She said she called the wall the Wall of Shame.

Those who give have faith that they will be rewarded in the near future, the distant future or after they pass away. The key is that they have faith. Are the people whose pictures hang on the Wall of Shame afraid of something? Are they afraid they won't receive recognition for their gifts? Are they afraid they've wasted their money? Do they need to realize immediate rewards in the form of recognition of their generosity? Do they feel this way every time they give?

Those who give anonymously understand that the universe will reciprocate. They don't need to see their faces on a wall, because they know they will be rewarded somewhere, sometime. Those who understand the concept of giving and its power are happy to give anonymously because they know that any form of giving will be repaid to them. We aren't always given credit for what we've done, but if the only thing that giving has provided you with is a good feeling, that's good enough. That feeling carries you through life. Whether it gives you greater confidence or simply puts a smile on your face, giving takes you to a higher level than you could reach if you didn't give. When we give, we carry with us a little secret—that we have given. We don't know when, but the universe will repay us. That knowledge alone should give you reason to get out of bed in the morning.

Giving to Those Who Know the Secret of Giving

Imagine two children playing a game of hot potato on a playground. Now picture two adults, both of whom understand the secret of giving, playing the same game. "I don't want your gifts. I want to be the one who gives," one says. The other gets angry and then throws the hot potato back. "No, I want to give," he says, and on and on it goes. These are the best relationships to be in because they're composed of two people who know that giving has power. Both parties dislike taking and love to give because they know which the universe favors.

Does your whole family regularly get together with other families? If you live in suburbia like I once did, you're probably familiar with this pastime. Whole families cram into one house, break bread and form relationships. Over time, you'll be able to tell if a family is a family of givers or takers. It's inevitable that some will turn out to be takers, but you just accept this and move on to the next family. My parents have taught me to be a member of a giving family. Don't wait for others to issue an invitation—it may never come. They may be waiting for *you* to strike up the friendship.

Just because someone is shy doesn't mean he isn't giving. Be the one to extend the invitation. The worst that could happen is that you have a well-attended meal.

WHO NOT TO GIVE TO

There are limits to the act of giving. Some of us have larger thresholds than others, but if you give too much, you spoil the opportunity to be on the receiving end. And sometimes you'll give to cheaters who take advantage of your generosity. I once invited such a person to stay at my home, and when he left, I decided to write him a letter but not to send it. Here is that letter:

> You came and you expected. Over the years I have shown you that I am willing to give. Given you a place to stay, food to eat, liquor to drink and all-around good times. This doesn't cost me much in the long run, but your not realizing and being thankful for it is a slap in the face. I would rather you say, "This one's on me," and buy me a meal. All I want is to not be taken advantage of and have reciprocation. If you can't see that, you just don't get it. Our ratio is well over five-to-one, and one gift or gesture will put us back in a more reasonable ratio.

WHEN TO GIVE

There are times when we don't want to give. We say to ourselves, "This giving won't benefit me at all. So I'll forgo this giving for giving in the future." But as we've seen, even giving something very small can have long-lasting effects. So when *should* we give? The answer to this question is personal. Some people give every day; others give only on special occasions. But if you think about giving in terms of more than just what you can get from it now and understand that it repays you forever, you may see the wisdom of giving more.

As I write this, it's July 2011, a time when the American economy is in a slump. Every day you read in the newspaper about some new problem concerning the national debt, America's central bank and the worthless bonds in some European countries. The global economy has been in a recession since 2008, and some people say there's no sign that things are picking back up. So, in these times, we want more from others. Those who have are supposed to give to those who have not, right?

No, they shouldn't be *expected* to. They worked hard for their money and can store it in a vault for the rest of their lives if they want to. But many people have become unemployed at an age when it's not practical to return to school and learn a new trade, and others in better economic positions want to help them. And that help will go a long way. During a recession, expectations of receiving money, or gifts, or luck are low, so, when you *do* give, the power of your gift is much greater than it would be during good economic times.

Consider the following scenario: John just got laid off from his job as a security guard at the local shopping mall. He'll receive a small severance package, but it won't be sufficient to feed his kids and pay his mortgage. Meanwhile, Martin's business has seen lower profits as a result of the recession, but he has savings in the bank and his wife has a stable job at a doctor's office. If you gave both John and Martin a gift of money, which one do you think would be more appreciative?

Besides giving because you know someone in need, another good reason to give is that it leads to a good reputation. If you don't give at all, your reputation will be a detriment to you, as others won't want to give to you and share with you because they realize they won't be reciprocated. You are missing out on many opportunities with others. To change that, you can factor giving into your lifestyle in the same way you factor saving money into your lifestyle. If you save 10 percent of your monthly or yearly income, set aside some of that for giving. You'll recoup your investment over and over. On the other hand, if you're too giving, your reputation can be that of someone who's easily taken advantage of. In that case, pull back the reins and let others reciprocate a little.

When Maimonides was in his early 20s, he and his family moved to Acre. After Jerusalem, Acre is politically the second city in the Latin Kingdom. Maimonides wrote, "I set sail from Morocco. And on the Sabbath, 10 Iyyar (April 24th) in the year 4925 AM (1165 CE), a great wave almost inundated us, the sea being very stormy. I took a vow that I would fast for these two days (every year) and observe them as a regular public fast, I and all my family and household."

In his time, Maimonides didn't have a smart phone to help him to organize his day and plan his life months in advance. In his head, he set days aside for performing certain activities, such as fasting and celebration. [22] If you set a day aside for giving—a certain day of the month or year—you'll be sure to give on that day. Pick a day that's important to you—your anniversary or the date of the death of a relative, for example.

Conversely, we must allow our giving to be harvested. If you give someone today or do something nice for someone today, you can't expect him to reciprocate immediately. Let your giving begin as a seed and wait until it blossoms into a tree that you can pick from when you need to. At times, we can give so much that it suffocates our seedlings; those we give to feel pressured to reciprocate in a way that they can't. Then they begin to resent both you and your generosity. As we saw in the beginning of the book, this pressure was the reason that ancient peoples such as the Au and the Gnau didn't accept gifts. The same phenomenon occurs today. Be cognizant of this.

WHAT TO GIVE

Let's assume you're giving to someone you know will give back to you. You've eliminated the possibility that he's a cheater, knowing him to be just the opposite, a reciprocator. What do you give him? There are millions of things you can give to others, tangible things like flowers and intangible things like your time, a compliment or a heartfelt smile. Usually, the things you like will also be liked by people who like *you*.

During a trip to Jerusalem, I saw religious men selling red thread outside the Western Wall. You were to take the red thread and turn it into a bracelet. I didn't know what the thread symbolized, but I liked the thought of having a souvenir from such a historic, holy place. When I returned home, I was complimented on my thin bracelet. When I visited Jerusalem again three years later, I bought 40 pieces of thread for 50 cents apiece and gave them away to people I care about. I told them the bracelets were good luck, and they were touched. As weeks passed, they continued to wear the bracelets, and I was touched because they respected my superstitions and took them to heart. A gift doesn't have to be expensive to be a good gift. The best gifts are the ones you put the most thought into. They're often from our spouses, our children or our good friends—the people we spend the most time with. When someone knows you very well and gives you something you like without asking you, it shows that the two of you are in sync.

It can be disappointing when someone asks you what you want for your birthday. For one thing, they aren't surprising you in any way, which prevents you from experiencing the feeling of elation you would otherwise have experienced. And they're allowing you to choose what you want. They aren't taking it upon themselves to analyze what you say and do and determine for themselves what you'd like. A gift card for a store you never shop at is one of the worst gifts people can give. It tells you the person who bought it for you doesn't know you very well and doesn't care enough to consider what you might like. Remember, the word *thoughtful* is associated with giving for a reason. The best gift is the one given with the most consideration of who we are.

GIVING TIME

Giving your time is one of the most genuine and rewarding forms of giving. It's also the most expensive, not monetarily but as an opportunity cost—the opportunity you're giving up by spending time doing something else. The potential for opportunity costs is infinite, and that's why our time is so valuable. Our worlds are filled with things to do. Most of us have jobs; some of us have kids. And we all have goals to pursue. We all want to take a vacation or spend time with our friends. How do we juggle all the millions of things in the world? The answer is, we can't. But we have to have a balance. We have to give to others while also giving to ourselves. Some people don't give enough to others and wonder why they're always alone. To these people, there's no time like the present to start giving to others, because if they do, they'll soon see the fruits of their generosity returned in the form of laughter and good company.

Giving your time can be as simple as volunteering at a hospital and talking with a lonely patient. And it will make *you* happier as well because when you walk out of the hospital, you'll feel a sense of purpose.

These feelings are priceless, and the more we give, the more we'll experience them.

And to prolong those feelings, we can give larger amounts of time, perhaps making dinner for your family or friends. This can take hours, and while you're cooking, setting the table and thinking about the smiles your loved ones will thank you with, you can start experiencing those good feelings before they've even arrived. Another way to prolong the pleasure is to prepare a surprise gift for someone to be delivered in a few weeks. You can think of the enjoyment they'll get from it long before it is delivered.

Giving Words

Words are powerful things. They can be used to motivate and they can be used to hinder.

Using words such as "You'll get better in no time" or "You're tough—you'll overcome this" can be used to help a friend heal after he's been injured. But words can also leave permanent scars, like when a parent constantly berates a child with words such as "You're dumb" and "You're ugly."

Giving words can lead to success not only for you but also for your child. Your words can encourage them. A parent who tells their children they can be whatever they want to be can have a significant impact on their success in life. Alternatively, a parent who scoffs at their children's dreams can affect them to the same degree.

A family friend once told me, "Kiss your kids so they'll kiss their kids." One might just as easily say, "Talk to your kids nicely so that they'll talk nicely to theirs." By building up your children's character, you encourage them to do whatever they desire and let them know they have your much-needed support. If you do this, they'll remember how you raised them. They'll use the character-building terms you said to them when they raise their own children. Just like with everything else we've learned about giving, the more you give with words, the more you get in return.

In the book *The Four Agreements*, author Miguel Ruiz compares word to seeds. You can plant seeds in people's brains with what you say to them. And *Think and Grow Rich* author Hill says of those who "give" negative words to others:

The person who, by word of mouth, gives expression to negative or destructive thoughts is practically certain to experience the results of those words in the form of a destructive 'kickback.' The first and perhaps the most important thing to remember is that the person who releases thoughts of a destructive nature must suffer damage through the breaking down of the faculty of creative imagination. Secondly, the presence in the mind of any destructive emotion develops a negative personality that repels people and often converts them into antagonists. The third source of damage to the person who entertains or releases negative thoughts lies in this significant fact—that these thought impulses are not only damaging to others, but they embed themselves in the subconscious mind of the person who releases them. They become part of their character. [23]... Unfortunately, there is no legal protection against those who, either by design or ignorance, poison the minds of others by negative suggestion. This form of destruction should be punishable by heavy legal penalties because it may and often does destroy one's chances of acquiring material things that are protected by law." [24]

Have you ever been running a negative thought through your mind for a while when someone suddenly says something to you that immediately turns your mood around? These moments are rare and exceptional. Why do people go to a priest or to a psychiatrist? Because they want to hear words that will help them, motivate them and, ultimately, make them feel better. It may cost you some money to see a psychiatrist, but many people find that it's worth it.

Giving Compliments and Receiving Criticism

The word *hello* is translated in the Mandarin language as *ni hao*. *Ni* means "you" and *hao* means "good." When you say "hello" to someone in Mandarin, essentially you're saying, "You are good." That's pretty nice if you think about it. So, like the Chinese, always give compliments. They boost people's egos. The more compliments you give to others, the more they'll like you and give you praise and compliments in return.

While giving compliments is easy, giving criticism is more difficult. In their book *Difficult Conversations*, authors Douglas Stone, Bruce Patton and Sheila Heen offer a few good tips for how to speak to someone you're mad at or frustrated with. First, be conscious of the direction in which you want to take the conversation. Don't start a fight for no reason. Rather, think long-term. Ask yourself, "Is this conversation worthwhile? If I look back on this moment in 10 years, will I still believe this exchange of words was necessary?" Second, tell the other person how you feel. Don't start the conversation by attacking him. If I said to you, "You know, you're always frowning. That's a bad quality," you'd probably get defensive. And ultimately, there would be no change in your character and my approach will only have garnered resentment.

Whenever you enter into a conversation, do so with the intention of learning something. Ask, "Is there something I can help you with? I notice sometimes that you're frowning." In this way, others feel open to vent to you as a caring friend. They won't feel criticized by you or view you as a judgmental outsider.

As much as we want to avoid confrontation, we must be negative at times. As I mentioned earlier in the book, the company or relationship that's all positive often fails because of a lack of preparation for negative unforeseen events. We may want to avoid negativity, but sometimes this is unwise. What to do? Dale Carnegie had an answer. He said it's best to precede criticism with a compliment. If someone reads this book and finds fault, the best way for him to tell me will be to say something like "I really admire your efforts in putting together this book. I thought it was well written. However, I thought it lacked...." This way you balance negative criticism with positive reinforcement and both are well received. If you provide only negative criticism, I'll be offended. I'll get defensive and miss the value of your words.

Giving Advice

When it comes to giving advice, you need to consider two things. First, who are you in comparison with the other person? Are you a 15-year old youth giving advice about marriage to a 40-year old adult? If so, be careful. Second, are you giving too much advice? If so, you risk becoming known as a know-it-all. Be a knowledge-giver just as often as you are a knowledge-taker. People want to give you their opinions, too.

Socrates gave his fellow Athenians advice and wisdom in his own way, now known as the Socratic Method. He'd discuss a subject with someone who held the opposite point of view and then question him over and over, forcing him to unwittingly contradict himself or agree with Socrates' viewpoint. This way, Socrates wasn't telling him what to think but letting him come to his own conclusions.

Giving Knowledge

On the reciprocation of knowledge, Dawkins' *Selfish Gene* is worth quoting again: "A relationship of mutual benefit between members of different species is called *mutualism* or *symbiosis*. Say, picking the ticks off a fellow but unrelated monkey. Problems arise if there is a delay between the giving of a favour and its repayment. This is because the first recipient of a favour may be tempted to cheat and refuse to pay it back when its turn comes." Like these monkeys, we remember those to whom we gave. We also remember those who either reciprocated or failed to do so. We don't want to be suckers and we want to punish the cheats. One can argue that we live in a society of mostly grudgers who are trying to eliminate the cheaters by not giving to them. And just like with the exchange of items, when sharing knowledge we must be careful that we're sharing with altruists or reciprocators.

Scientists aptly depict an altruistic culture of sharing knowledge. One scientist does research and writes a paper. He or she then allows other scientists to read it and use the data in future papers. Over time, their combined knowledge is collected into a pool of papers, all of them available for anyone to read.

The scientist who wrote the original paper expects nothing in return other than to be cited in subsequent papers as the source of the information. If he'd refused to let other scientists quote their paper, he could expect other scientists to do the same. The entire system is based on goodwill and sharing, and because of this relationship, science flourishes.

This concept works in countless other areas as well. Benjamin Franklin formed a club of intellectuals who met in his attic to discuss politics, religion and other matters and generally enlighten one another. Like the scientists, Franklin and his friends understood that giving up exclusive ownership of their knowledge would ultimately allow them access to more knowledge. If they didn't have this confidence, they wouldn't have shared with one another.

Giving to Yourself

Studies show that willpower, the ability to self-regulate, is a learned concept we gain when we're very young. Psychologist Walter Mischel did a famous study on willpower with 4-year-olds and marshmallows in the late 1960s. He gave the preschoolers the choice of eating one marshmallow now or waiting 15 minutes and getting two. When he followed up decades later, he found that the 4-year-olds who waited for two marshmallows turned into adults who were better adjusted, were less likely to abuse drugs, had higher self-esteem, had better relationships, were better at handling stress, obtained higher degrees and earned more money. [25]

But can willpower be learned later in life? Is there hope for those of us who can't stick to a diet? For those who want to quit smoking or drinking but haven't been able to? For those who want to embark on a particular career but can't get started? How can we learn willpower and drive ourselves to accomplish things? The answer lies in giving—giving to ourselves.

We have to give to our future selves and delay gratification. There's scientific proof that we actually derive pleasure from delaying gratification. Studies have shown that expectation itself is a source of happiness because you don't derive pleasure only from the expected event—you also experience pleasure by looking forward to it. Even if the event itself is a disappointment, the expectation isn't. Those who devote time to looking forward to enjoyable experiences report that they're happier in general. [26] But if you're looking forward to a party or a vacation, beware: The higher your expectations, the more dissapointed you'll be if it doesn't turn out as you'd have liked.

Studies have also shown that people who keep gratitude journals are happier, more energetic and have a better sense of well being than those who don't. [27] The optimal amount of time to set aside for practicing gratitude is once a week, and it's best to reflect on three events, places or objects. This may be because if we're grateful all the time, we'll water down the value of each event or object.

Every Sunday night, write down three things you're grateful for. They can be as simple as family members, friends and pets or more abstract things like the smell of the outdoors. In time you'll notice the little things in life and be more grateful for them because you're habitually looking for them to write down in your weekly journal.

American psychiatrist and award-winning author Peter Whybrow says our brains have two parts, the lizard brain and the mammalian brain. Our mammalian brain is the part that grows with learning and education. It's our superego, the part of the brain that controls our desires and self-regulates. The lizard brain is the part that wants to eat, sleep and have sex—our id. In American culture, Whybrow says, the lizard brain has taken over. With constant advertisements to buy and consume and with everything at our fingertips, we've lost the ability to control our selves. He says Americans' indebtness levels and obesity levels are almost exactly the same.

It's clear that we need more self-regulation. We have to delay gratification sometimes. Basic math is thoroughly covered in schools, but we don't learn how to save early enough. If we did, we'd be much more likely to do so. One of the best books on the topic of personal finance is *The Wealthy Barber*, by David Chilton. It discusses the idea of arranging for the automatic deposit of 10 percent of your company paycheck directly into a savings account. He uses the term *pay yourself first.* This is a great way to ensure that you always give to your future self. There are also great software applications such as HelloWallet™ and Mint™ that can help you save money as you monitor your day-to-day spending habits and plan for your future.

Plans of any kind take time. We can't become the president of the United States as soon as we graduate from university, nor can we become a great athlete without investing the necessary hard work, dedication and persistence. The people who succeed are those who map out their goal and remain true to it. They don't waver when times got tough—they persist. Giving can help us to persist in many ways. When you support friends and family members who are down in the dumps by offering a shoulder to cry on, they'll be there to support you when the roles are reversed. By giving now, you ensure that you'll be given to in the future.

We can also give ourselves compliments and positive encouragement, which help us to muster the strength to carry on. If you didn't sign the deal you thought you would, or if you got robbed and now have to dip into your holiday savings account, how do you remain optimistic? Whenever you have a rough day, say 10 positive things about your life. Give yourself the sweet taste of positivity. The more good things you do in your life and the more accomplishments and successes you have, the more you can recall them when you need to give yourself a pep talk. You can also turn failures into positives with words. *Overcoming obstacles, growing,* and *learning from my failures* are phrases we can lavish on ourselves when something hasn't gone the way we wanted.

And what about people who "bring us down," maybe your ex-girlfriend or the boss who always seems to kibosh everything you propose? Whenever you find yourself thinking about these people, think instead about all the people who influence your life in a positive way. Name 10 of them—perhaps your mother, father, best friend, sister, brother, grandparent, the barista who serves you coffee every morning, or the sweet woman from Federal Express you just talked to on the phone. There are more people in this world whom you like and who also like you, than there are those who maybe had a bad day, or a bad childhood, and are punishing the rest of us. Focus on those good people. Name them as often as you can. The more people you're good to and are in harmony with, the more of these people you can call on when your spirits are in need of raising.

When we can think positively in spite of negative circumstances, we persevere. People who persevere can overcome obstacles and make something of themselves. When we are able to maintain a high positive ratio, we're able to achieve the American Dream or a happy marriage or a general feeling of well being. When we watch and read the news, especially during recession or war, we can dig a hole of negativity. To dig out of that hole, we need a positive mind-set. And yes, that's easier said than done, but maybe not as hard as you think. Your mind and body are actually more responsive to what *you* give them than to what *other people* give them. Within your own mind and body, there are no cheaters and no takers, so the reciprocation is guaranteed.

In his book *Secrets of Abundant Wealth*, Adam Jackson maintains that charity is one of the secrets to maintaining a high positive ratio. To illustrate his point, he uses the allegory of two brothers who desperately want to go to school to become artists. Their family is too poor to send them both, though, and the boys flip a coin to see who will go and who will pay for the schooling by working in the mines. The plan is that after four years they'll switch roles. The younger brother wins, studies hard and becomes a great artist. When he returns home and tells his brother that he'll now work to pay for *his* schooling, the older brother holds up his hands, which are now arthritic and stiff, and says, "I cannot become an artist any longer. Working in the mines has crippled me. I am happy for you, though, brother, and happy to have helped you become the man you are."

The brothers represent the past and the future. The older brother is the former you. He needs to make a sacrifice for his younger brother, the one who has more time ahead of him. His sacrifice will allow his brother to go to school and realize greatness. To get what it wants for its future, your present self can either do nothing or sacrifice something. Don't waste time. The younger brother is waiting and your past is getting arthritic hands. To realize greatness in life, sacrifices need to be made.

The book *Creating Your Best Life,* by Caroline Adams Miller and Dr. Michael B. Frisch, teaches the principles of creating life goals so you can get the most out of life. It's about giving to yourself—challenging yourself to be better in relationships, work, finances and every other aspect of your life. It helped me define my life goals and what I wanted to accomplish in my short time on Earth. I hung my list of goals on the wall and read them almost daily, and now they're either coming true or have already come true. (Incidentally, Miller is one of the first graduates of the groundbreaking Master of Applied Positive Psychology program offered at the University of Pennsylvania—the program Martin Seligman created as an in-depth study of the science of well-being.)

Setting goals and being constantly motivated to achieve aren't for everyone. You may be content with where you are in life, but if you want to raise the bar, make a goal list. It's the best gift you can give yourself. If you do, and if you read the book *Creating Your Best Life*, in five years you'll find that everything you wrote down will have been accomplished. This is how the law of attraction works.

Jason Terry is a player on the Dallas Mavericks basketball team. In 2011, before his team had passed the first round of the playoffs, Terry tattooed an image of the world-championship trophy on his arm. Obtaining the trophy was his goal and he'd settle for nothing less. So in his own way, he asked the universe to give it to him. He was prepared to receive it, and he and his team won the world championship that year.

Here are a few good websites that teach the art of goal-setting:

- 101 things in 1000 days.com
- 43things.com
- mygoals.com
- goal enforcer.com
- mylifechanges.com
- mindtools.com
- joesgoals.com
- solidgoals.com
- justgiving.com

When you make plans or goals, the way you phrase them in your head is important. You need to use the present tense, so instead of saying, "I will be a great businessman," or "I will be a great friend," say, "I am a great friend," or "I am a great businessman." This way you place yourself as the main character in the attainment of your goal, and in your mind you've already begun working toward it. Your goals shouldn't be too lofty, though. Don't say, "I am making $2 million this year," because you might be disappointed. Instead say, "I am making a lot of money this year." Woody Allen said, "I wanted to be an actor and became one. I wanted to be a comedian and director and I became one. Everything I aspired to in my life has come true. So why do I still feel I got screwed?" We can ask and we can receive, but when we receive, we need to realize that we're wired to crave more, to continue craving and not becoming idle. Don't stop asking from the universe, because if you do, you'll become unfocused, bored and disillusioned.

Giving to Your Body

Medical doctors and naturopaths will tell you that your body is like a machine. If you fuel it correctly, it will run smoothly. To quote my friend Maimonides again, he said that if we feed ourselves with the same thought and care with which we feed our herd, we won't become ill. Just like with giving to your friends or strangers, the benefits of giving to your body won't always materialize immediately. Rather, you see the benefits when you feel fit enough to go on that long bike ride or when someone says to you, "You look good. Have you been working out?"

Give to your body by exercising and eating well. Working out is good for your health and your body chemistry, and it also builds confidence. When you leave the gym, you can say to yourself, "I went—I have discipline. I went—I'm in good shape. I went—I can do anything I want. I did 15 push-ups—I'm strong. I rode the bike for 15 minutes—I have endurance." It's not necessarily the results that get us going back to the gym but the positivity we get by being disciplined enough to go.

Many people exercise to lose weight. They walk or run on a treadmill for hours, but they don't see the results. That's because the best way to lose weight is to burn muscle. We're burning some muscle when we use the treadmill, but not in the same way we burn muscle when we lift weights or do crunches, push-ups and other simple workouts. These activities help us to lose weight because, the next day, while our muscles still burn and ache, our bodies try to repair and rebuild themselves. In the process, they burn energy and, in turn, shed fat. You're gaining the benefits of working out without working out. Like with the other forms of giving, by working out today, we can reap the benefits tomorrow.

Giving to Your Mind

There are people who go through their whole lives saying negative words to themselves because of seeds planted in their minds at a young age. They started life thinking they weren't smart, attractive or worthy of love. As adults, they continue to berate themselves, as though they have a bully living inside their head. It is a part of human nature to be realistic about the world but this sometimes translates into us having pessimistic thoughts such as "how can you become president, there is not enough time, you're not smart enough, you're too old".

In his book *Authentic Happiness*, Seligman identifies two kinds of people. The first uses temporary self-talk during negative moments and permanent self-talk during positive moments. The second does the opposite. Let's use Sally and Keith as examples. If Sally were involved in a car accident, she might say to herself, "Oh well, this is a rare occurrence and just an accident." Keith would say to himself, "I'm dumb. I always do stupid things. My ex was right—I'm a loser." Sally uses temporary self-talk to get herself through the incident, while the Keith beats himself up over it.

If Sally were given a promotion at work, she might say to herself, "I deserve this promotion. I work hard and achieve everything in my life that I set out to achieve." If Keith were given a promotion, he might say to himself, "This is just luck. My boss must have been in a good mood this month." This time, Sally uses permanent self-talk to congratulate herself, while Keith uses temporary self-talk. Not surprisingly, Seligman found in his studies that people like Sally are happier people. Talk to yourself the way a best friend or a loving parent would talk to you.

Seligman also wrote *Flourish*, which discusses the idea of positive psychology, the basis for the Master of Applied Positive Psychology program. The MAPP course teaches us to talk to ourselves and to others in ways that make us flourish. The key exercise is as follows:

Think back to what you did yesterday. Name three good things that happened to you. How did they make you feel? What strength in your character made them happen? How can they be made to happen more often? This can be something as small as doing the laundry or something as big as getting a promotion. For example, "I drove to pick up my friends and then the three of us went out for lunch. I am a great driver who has the intelligence to drive a vehicle from my house to their houses with ease. I am independent enough to do anything I want in life. I have close friends who care about me because I care about them. I am a kind, empathetic person. My friends know they can come to me with their issues and problems, just like I can go to them with mine. I am a shoulder they can cry on."

When you get into this habit of talking yourself up, it becomes a part of you. And according to Seligman, you flourish because of it. The more positive things we do in our lives, the more goals we achieve; the more accomplishments to our credit, the more material we have for talking positively to ourselves. Say you're working for a company you hate. The owners are unethical, some of their actions may be illegal and you hate the way they treat you and your co-workers. After much thought, you decide to quit even though you'll be out of work. You can be proud of yourself for maintaining your integrity and your values. Whenever you question yourself, you can use this example to reassure yourself that you're a strong and bold person.

We need to love ourselves with positive words, talk ourselves up and treat ourselves in the same way that a coddling mother or a best friend would. I'm not saying you should change your psyche immediately, but once every few hours, try saying three good things about yourself. Put a reminder on your phone that activates every few hours to remind you to tell yourself three good things about yourself. The results will surprise you.

TIME + EFFORT = SUCCESS

I've read many articles about how my generation is spoiled. Rumor has it that a) we expect to find a good job at a good company and be paid a good salary as soon as we graduate from university, and that b) we're going to suffer a greater rate of depression and quit more jobs than any generation before us. To those who are older than us and think this is the case, is that so bad? Didn't you tell us to reach for the stars and, in the worst case, hit the moon? You say we aren't going to be happy until we reach a level in our careers where we're making a difference in the world. Is it not better to want to achieve such a goal than to have no goals at all?

Both Malcolm Gladwell's *Outliers* and Geoff Colvin's *Talent Is Overrated* say the people who are successful in their careers are the people who have invested the most time into them. Gladwell calls it the "10,000-hour rule." Experts in a given field, be it chess, music, sports or computers, have all invested 10,000 hours into it. As a result, they're able to perform at the highest level. They can quickly make correct assumptions on matters related to their industry and have created some of the greatest music, programs or careers in all of history.

We get back what give we give to ourselves and more. Look at your career like a well that needs to be filled with water. You need to fill the well with hours of learning and reading and many ups and downs in order to have a steady supply of water. Because it evaporates, we need to be constantly replenishing it.

Why are we so surprised when the class valedictorian is struggling in his 40s while a picture of the class clown, who was voted most likely to fail, appears on the cover of *Fortune* magazine? What has happened is that the valedictorian rested on the laurels of his "genius" and his valedictorianesque capabilities, failing to understand that life is a marathon, not a sprint. Clearly, his effort and drive have waned as the years went on, or perhaps he hasn't found the right industry. As for the class clown, sometimes people don't do well in high school but begin to love learning and education once they've attended a few years of university, and sometimes this doesn't even begin until we're in our 30s.

People who understand and value the concept that what you put in you'll get back tenfold see their efforts come back to them, in terms of both money and career satisfaction. They understand time and effort and the mathematics behind them—that their efforts compound over time. You will know to learn more and more and be patient in seeing the forthcoming results.

The successful have faith that when they learn something, it will pay dividends. They're convinced that they should constantly educate themselves, demanding to learn more because they realize that people are born with a certain intelligence but that it's effort and time that make someone well read, educated and on top of trends. Intelligent people with no faith in learning remain smart but often miss out on opportunities to advance themselves.

These experts become experts not only by practicing for 10,000 hours but also by practicing the right way. This concept, formulated by Dr. K. Anders Ericsson, a psychology professor at Florida State University, is known as deliberate practice. If you're a trying to become a pro at something, you often hit plateaus you can't get past. To overcome obstacles, Ericsson says, you have to focus on getting better at your biggest weakness. In his book, *Moonwalking with Einstein*, Joshua Foer learns to become a memorization expert. When he hits a plateau, he gets help from not only other experts at memory competition but from Ericson himself. He instructs Foer to focus more time and energy on the activities in which he's getting the worst times and scores. Foer heeds his advice and goes on to turn in a great performance at the U.S. memory competition.

In Canada, becoming an oral surgeon is a difficult goal to attain. Only a handful of students are accepted into the program, and not only must they have great marks, but they must also have the nerve to rack up a hefty student loan because the program is eight years in length. Benji, a friend of my father's, knew at age 20 that he wanted to become a oral surgeon, so he went to New York and asked an oral surgeon there if he would allow him to work in the office without having to pay him a penny! Astounded, the doctor accepted his offer. As a result, Benji got his foot in the door. Once he completed his degree, he was then able to practice as an oral surgeon because he received the necessary hours of on-site training. This is an example of how thinking long term about your career and seeing it as a well can benefit you when you need to drink its water. Many students refuse to work for free in great internships. They don't understand that this can propel them leaps and bounds ahead of their fellow students. Instead, they accept a position that pays them a large salary but doesn't teach them much. But if they'd accepted that unpaid internship and looked 10 years into the future, they'd see themselves working for a great company under great management. They'd see a person who is much further ahead than the one who chose the high-paying job. At 20 years of age, Benji was able to look into his future, and he's now one of Toronto's leading oral surgeons.

Recently I noticed that my 15-year-old cousin was working on a school assignment that asked, "How do the members of *Jersey Shore* abuse the idea of partying?" She'd written that they go out every night and lead a lifestyle of looking good and drinking and having sex. When I asked her why she thought that was bad, she said that she likes the idea of going out on the weekends but that if you go out every night, the novelty is lost. When I asked why it's acceptable to party on the weekends, she said it's a reward for your hard work during the week.

Whether you party or not, when you work hard at something—when you put in the hours required to produce something of value—you can be proud of yourself. And then when you do reward yourself you feel you have earned it.

Reading

Reading books is a great investment to make in your personal knowledge base. It helps you to stay abreast of trends and find ways to become creative in your life.

Reading compounds knowledge because after you read something, you can test its validity in the external world. If it turns out to be true, you'll embrace this particular truth and be better off for it.

Another benefit of education and reading is that, you see the results in your vocabulary. This improves your ability to hold a conversation with an intellectual uncle and is more likely to impress during your dream-job interview. And this will lead you to want to learn even more. In fact, I believe people can become addicted to learning. When a person experiences the benefits of reading a good book, he craves another book. But it's OK—it's a good addiction to have.

To the human brain, knowledge is fuel. Most successful people are readers. If you research the life of a president or a successful entrepreneur, it's almost guaranteed that you'll discover that they accumulated a massive library of books. Thomas Jefferson's library included 6,487 books. [28] Abraham Lincoln would travel to a neighboring village at the age of 9 just to find a book that was available there. [29] Lincoln, who was president only a few months before the start of the Civil War, and he knew nothing of battle, but he read as much as he could about the subject, including the war tactics of Napoleon and Sun Tzu. Ultimately, his newfound knowledge helped the Union defeat the Confederates. In fact, Lincoln went through four generals because after reading about war, he became an expert on it and knew what he needed in a general to be victorious.

Another fanatical reader was Theodore Roosevelt. It's said that he would read 500 books in a single year—that's almost 10 books a week. This is a passage from his biography by Edmund Morris:

> Somewhere between six one evening and eight thirty next morning, beside his dressing and his dinner and his guests and his sleep, he had read a volume of three hundred and odd pages, and missed nothing of significance that it contained."
> "On evenings, when he has no official entertaining to do, Roosevelt will read two or three book entire. His appetite for titles is omnivorous and insatiable, ranging from the histories of Thucydides to the tales of Uncle Remus. Reading, as he has explained to Trevelyan is for him the purest imaginative therapy.

Albert Einstein was also a voracious reader. He was reading books about complicated mathematics at the age of 10. By the time he was 12, he understood the philosophy of Immanuel Kant, something that many *adults* aren't capable of. One of Einstein's many famous quotes is "I believe that love is a better teacher than duty."

Another man who owes his success partly to reading is Seymour Schulich, a wealthy entrepreneur who made his fortune in the mining industry. Schulich started Toronto's Schulich School of Business, one of the world's best business schools. In his biography,

Get Smarter: Life and Business Lessons, he said he'd read more than 5,000 books in his life.

Kevin O'Leary, the mean guy on the reality-TV series *Dragons' Den*, says in his autobiography that his stepfather told him to get an MBA when he was in his early 20s. The more a person learns and experiences, he said, the more he has in his toolbox of life. I would add that voracious reading belongs in your toolbox, too. In the same way that lifting weights gives to our muscles, reading gives to our minds. The men and women who win weight-lifting contests are those who are the strongest and train the hardest. The same rule can be applied to success in life. You have to train your mind. There are a million ways to give to yourself, and just like with the other forms of giving, you have to think long term when giving to yourself. You'll see that nothing responds better to giving than your mind and your body.

Once again, we've seen that those who are successful are those who have faith that what they do will pay off. Abraham Lincoln might not have known he was destined to become president, and Albert Einstein didn't know what kind of mark he would leave on science and history, but they did understand that because of all of the knowledge they accumulated through study and hard work, something important was going to happen to them.

WHAT WE LEAVE BEHIND

When you're gone from this world, all that's left is your legacy. Memories of how you behaved in both business and your personal life will mix together like clothes in a washing machine and be hung on the line for all to consider. So always be thinking about your legacy as a gestalt of your whole life, not just your business history or your personal life. How can you leave a strong mark on the world by giving today and later, from your grave?

Life moves quickly. We're in our bodies for the blink of an eye. There have been billions of people who have come into the world and left it without leaving a mark. Andrew Carnegie said, "The man who dies rich dies disgraced," and, "He who gives while he lives also knows where it goes."

If you want to be remembered, the surest way to keep yourself in someone's thoughts is to produce offspring. Your progeny will continue your genetic makeup, and at the very least they'll ask about you in family-tree conversations. But what if you want to leave a legacy not only for your children but for the rest of the world? To leave this kind of legacy, you have to be forward-thinking. You have to think ahead many generations and ask not "How will I be remembered?" but "How can I be remembered"?

The best way to leave a great legacy is to represent something, to be yourself and live life as genuinely as you can. Did Abraham Lincoln or Mother Teresa do what they did in life in order to attain fame or leave a mark on the world? We can't know for sure, but it's probably safe to assume they did it because it felt right.

Close your eyes for a moment and picture your great- great-grandparents. Do you even know who they were? If you do, that's great, but you probably don't know who *their* great-great-grandparents were or where they came from. Where were your genes 1,000 years ago? The point I'm trying to make is that it's hard to leave a legacy. If your goal is to be remembered by your future family members, deposit $100 in a bank account and let it mature in 50 or 100 or 500 years. You'll be remembered by your offspring for a few generations, but not for much longer.

My late grandmother and grandfather would buy me 10-year Israeli bonds for my birthday every year. I still receive the principal and interest from some of these bonds in the mail and when I do, I think fondly of my grandparents. Although it wasn't much, their giving prompts me to reflect on them more than I otherwise might. But that's not why I remember them, and it's not why I'll tell my own grandchildren about them. I remember them for the way they lived their lives and the relationship I had with them. My grandparents had a loving marriage and a desire for knowledge. My grandfather survived the Holocaust, and my grandmother was a great mother and grandmother. Those are the things I remember most about them. Legacies are not about leaving behind tangibles—they're about leaving behind intangibles.

Legacies can also amount to the passing on of knowledge. Many cultures, namely the indigenous peoples of the desert, the arctic and the jungle, all learn how to hunt prey (and how to avoid becoming prey) from their ancestors. Knowing how to build an igloo, harvest mussels and kill whales in the arctic isn't something you come up with on your own. It has to be passed down from your forefathers. Just like knowledge of poisonous jungle plants, some of which can be used to enhance hunting and some of which are dangerous to handle. And an understanding of how to dig wells and connect them so they produce more water flow, which is essential in the African desert.

Our lifestyles may be worlds apart from indigenous peoples who live off the land, but establishing the basics for a legacy are the same in any world. A basic legacy is left by teaching the next generation the right way and the wrong way. This will never change as long as the human race continues to exist.

A perfect example of legacy-building is the Living Bridge. In Cherrapunju, Meghalaya, which is in northern India, a community has built a bridge entirely from the roots of living trees. The roots take time to strengthen, and generation after generation must continue to build the bridge. Fathers must teach their children how so that they, in turn, can teach their children. The tree is physical evidence of the legacy of forefathers who have laid the foundation for their offspring.

Another way to leave our mark is to add things to the world that can be appreciated 100 or 1,000 years from now. Giving money is the easiest way to do this, but you can also leave behind your ideas. Write your memoirs or a book of your insights, make movies, or keep journals. Write down your opinions for future generations to enjoy and learn from. As Pat Williams said in his book *Reading for Your Life*, when you read a book you're gaining someone else's knowledge—knowledge gained over a lifetime.

Of course, writing is only one suggestion for leaving your mark on the world. Neither Jesus nor Buddha left any written word about their philosophies and beliefs, but they made indelible impressions just the same. Maybe they made such a mark *because* the edicts weren't written down and were instead allowed to take on lives of their own through their passing down.

Another way to leave legacies is through our businesses. If you run your own business, don't build it just for your survival. Build it on an ideology that can be carried for generations. I once read about a pencil company in Germany whose owners were eighth-generation—the man who started the company is still remembered eight generations later. If you build companies to which others can contribute, you can lay the foundation for a family business that continues to thrive long after you're gone. However, like many things, your wishes can backfire. If your shoes are too big to fill, your success can kill your children's drive and determination. When it comes to business, we must ensure that we build a business that our offspring can believe in and that they can put their own passions into without fear of being compared with us.

That goes for politics, too. Politicians who are assassinated are often succeeded by their wives, sons or daughters. This is because these loved ones are often as impassioned about improving lives and other causes as the deceased leaders were.

Aung San fought for the democracy of Burma and was assassinated at age 32. Now he's a legend in Burma. Statues of him preside over the streets, and he's depicted on the one-kyat bill. His daughter, Aung San Suu Kyi, was two years old when he was assassinated, and the people of Burma later persuaded her to assume her father's destiny and transform Burma into a democracy. She did so with passion and bravery, but after her National Democratic League political party won the election, the militaristic government ordered her to nearly 20 years of house arrest. Although a fair vote had been cast to elect a democratic government, her people's wishes for democracy were not fulfilled. Until only recently, as I write this, her party has just won 43 of the 45 seats in the house of parliament.

If we want to be remembered, we need to leave behind something for our children to follow. Aung San Suu Kyi's story illustrates this beautifully. A belief in your philosophies, coupled with the passion to spread or abide by them, will allow your loved ones not only to remember you but to live lives greatly influenced by you. I suppose that my writing of this little book is my way of showing my belief in the beliefs of my own father.

In one of the final episodes of the television series *Entourage*, the character Vince falls in love with a gorgeous British reporter, but he can't seem to make her want him the same way he's done with women in past episodes. His closest friends, Turtle and Johnny Drama (also his half-brother), get in touch with her and tell her how great Vince is. Turtle tells her about the time Vince secretly paid off his family's mortgage because they were about to be evicted. Johnny tells her Vince will do anything for him. Although Vince is a fictional character, he illustrates the concept of performing giving acts that people will continue to talk about. When you give, people just might tell others that you're the best person they've ever known.

In his famous book *Meditations*, Marcus Aurelius looked at the idea of living life to leave a legacy as foolish. He wrote:

> He who has a vehement desire for posthumous fame does not consider that every one of those who remember him will himself also die very soon; then again also they who have succeeded them, until the whole remembrance shall have been extinguished as it is transmitted through men who foolishly admire and perish. But suppose that those who will remember are even immortal, and that the remembrance will be immortal, what then is this to thee? And I say not what is it to the dead, but what is it to the living? What is praise except indeed so far as it has a certain utility? For thou now rejectest unseasonably the gift of nature, clinging to something else. [30]

What good is posthumous fame if the people who remember you will also be gone one day? What's the value of being remembered if you're gone? The answers lie in altruism. If we live a life that others can admire and talk about, in which we not only gave and sacrificed but enjoyed life too, we leave the living with guidance on how to lead similar lives. And we get value from it ourselves in the form of knowledge—the knowledge that we've made a contribution to the world.

Today

We're going to live longer, visit more countries and meet more people than any generation before, not to mention all the people we'll correspond with on Facebook or follow on Twitter.

If you were a caveman and you met another caveman, you wouldn't know if you'd ever see him again and you'd have to choose between killing him and befriending them. Attempting to kill him would put your life at risk, so sharing with him or giving him gifts would be the wiser choice. Whether the other caveman would make the same choice is another story, of course. Today, we like to think we're more civilized, and there's certainly less reason to resort to violence, but we still have to make a decision about how to behave when we meet a new person. Will we be rude or will we be cordial? Will we take or give?

Maybe the best way to sum up the concept of giving is with the lyrics to the song in a certain Coca-Cola® commercial: "You give a little love and it all comes back to you. La la la la la la la la. You're going to be remembered for the things that you say and do." The tune is merely catchy, but the message is resounding: Give, give and don't be afraid to give some more.

AFTERWORD

Midnight in Paris is a brilliant Woody Allen movie about a lost and struggling writer (played by Owen Wilson) who travels back in time to Paris in the 1920s. While he's there, he meets many successful writers and artists, among them the famous poet Gertrude Stein. She tells Wilson's character, "We all fear death and our place in the universe. The job of the author is to give hope. Don't be such a defeatist."

I hope that after reading this book, you understand the act of giving a little better and realize that there's reason for hope. Freud believed that the way to happiness is to experience less misery. Putting an end to your depression and angst was the best you could hope for in his time. But Martin Seligman says that we can not only eliminate our misery and depression but also improve our well-being and flourish through giving. He uses the acronym *PERMA* to explain the five things we need in our lives in order to do that: [31]

P—Positive emotion (feeling good—i.e., getting a massage, eating good food)

E—Engagement (being in flow—doing work you love and can become consumed by)

R—Relationships (loving marriages, close friendships)

M—Meaning (finding a higher purpose for why you are here)

A—Accomplishments (setting goals for yourself and achieving them)

As we've learned from studies discussed in this book, giving feels good, so through the act of giving, you can achieve positive emotion (P). When we devote hours to the challenges of our careers, we can reach new heights and achieve engagement (E). By giving, you can improve your existing relationships (R) and find new ones that are reciprocal and long-lasting. When it comes to accomplishments (A), patience is often the key. We need to steadily put forth the effort to achieve our goals while always remembering that things don't come back to us today. By laying out a clear plan for yourself in all facets of your life, you can find yourself flourishing.

I believe that, of the five criteria that Seligman has

listed, meaning (M) is the most difficult to achieve. Some people's purpose is to *find* meaning. For others, meaning is already understood, as Lao Tzu says and The Beatles famously sing in the song *Inner Light:*

Without going out of my door
I can know all things on earth.
Without looking out of my window
I could know the ways of heaven.
The farther one travels,
The less one knows.

In some ways, life becomes easier as we gain knowledge. But in a very significant way, it actually becomes more challenging as we go along. The more we learn, the harder we try to find purpose in our lives. As we become wealthier, smarter and healthier, we climb Maslow's hierarchy of needs, ranging from basic needs like shelter to advanced needs like self-actualization. Our needs grow as we do.

There are highly intelligent people who know a lot about the universe. They know about the stars, about black holes and about Einstein's Theory of Relativity. But even Stephen Hawking, the leading expert on these topics, says in his book *A Brief History of Time* that not even he knows the answer to the question "Why?" Why are we here? Why is this universe the way it is? What's the purpose? We'll never know. But what we do know is that since we're here, we might as well give. In return, besides joy, laughter and companionship, we get self-esteem and self-actualization when we give to ourselves or to the MA (meaning and accomplishment) in Seligman's PERMA acronym. While we don't know the purpose of the universe, we *can* discover our own purpose, and to do that we have to give something, whether it's the effort required to become a better athlete, the passing on of knowledge to make the world a better place, or the sharing of our time in order to touch as many hearts as we can touch. Once you choose your purpose and your meaning, start working toward it and don't ever stop.

Through the act of giving, I have given you many messages in this book. The last message in this little book is similar to Victor Frankl's message in the classic book *Man's Search for Meaning*. He said that if you find a higher calling, you will live your life with purpose. Frankl's own calling happened to be telling and teaching people about the importance of finding meaning in life. We should represent something in this world. Once you find your calling, pass it on to the next generation. Are you a teacher? Then your calling is to give knowledge. Are you a businessman? Then you fill a need that people have. Are you a politician? Then you hope to make a difference for people. Are you without a career or a purpose? Think about what you want to give, what you want to leave to the world and to your children. Work backward and determine what you want to represent, and then go after it!

We all want success. We want to leave our mark on the world. And through giving, we *can*. Givers will leave their mark. According to many religions, after we leave this world, all our actions follow us into the next. Think of your actions as the words printed on a T-shirt. What do those words say about you. What do you stand for?

Giving has always been a topic of conversation in my household because my mother and father have always been generous people. My mother, who is a children's hygienist, is popular in the community. She asks her patients about their lives and genuinely cares about what they have to say and how they're doing. For over 20 years, people have booked appointments with my mother as much as six months in advance. Children she saw in the earliest days of her practice still book appointments with her even though they aren't children anymore. I asked her why gives so much, and she said, "Because I know how I feel when others give to me." She feels happy when she gives.

My father is constantly giving to those who have less. I noticed a connection between his personality and the personalities of others who are successful: They give. And perseverance and patience are an inextricable part of the package. The giver's mentality includes the determination to weather the storms and an ability to see far down the road.

Paul, a feng shui expert, my family and I have consulted in decorating our office and homes, once told me, "Don't listen to the negative people in the world and the doubters. There are only a very few successful people in the world. If you listen to everyone, you will be surely listening to those who have failed or are bitter." To be successful, we need to persevere. We need to get up after we're knocked down. Giving adds a degree of support to our lives because when you give, you get good karma and the assurance that when *you* need something, you could ask for it—a comfort when times are tough. Additionally, by talking positively to ourselves, cheering ourselves on and taking care of ourselves, we become unstoppable.

Make no mistake—giving is difficult and can take us out of our way. Telling your parents how much they mean to you, giving a donation to a charity and exercising all require effort. But make no mistake about *this* either—the rewards are worth the efforts.

In writing this book, I wanted to make sense of giving and find out if it was, in fact, as powerful as I was led to believe. I learned that it is, and I also understand why. By giving, I'm able to foster harmonious relationships with those I care about and at the same time represent something I believe is important to humanity. Giving has thus helped provide my life with its meaning. It's also fostered the belief that I can accomplish anything. I hope this book has fostered the same belief for you.

NOTES

[1] *If money doesn't make you happy, then you probably aren't spending it right*, Elizabeth W. Dunn, Daniel T. Gilbert, Timothy D. Wilson University of British Columbia

[2] Journal references: *Science*, vol 319, p 1687; *Review of General Psychology*, vol 9, p 111-131)

[3] news.sciencemag.org

[4] Great Courses Effective Communication Skills Taught By Professor Dalton Kehoe, Ph.D., York University,

[5] *Workplace sabotage fueled by envy, unleashed by disengagement*: UBC research, The University of British Columbia, October 6, 2011

[6] Make or break? Social networking tames cheats, *The Economist*, November 19, 2011

[7] The Role of Gossip, Reputation and Charisma in Inducing Cooperation, *Social Science Research Network*, April 1, 2007

[8] http://books.google.ca/books?id=44r9DSS8KLkC&pg=PA181&lpg=PA181&dq=marcel+israel+mauss+gift&source=bl&ots=rAEoGwOewm&sig=bTlhk2u7wuBGJLD_XswsXPbuyQI&hl=en&sa=X&ei=4EwTT9KuAsXx0gG3mbSKAw&ved=0CGoQ6AEwBw#v=onepage&q=marcel%20israel%20mauss%20gift&f=false

[9] http://books.google.ca/books?id=b2BUEXDRfWgC&pg=PA84&lpg=PA84&dq=au+and+gnau+gifting&source=bl&ots=u0P36nfylf&sig=l51v6WJEelTU1JAqKXpAO3O0L_I&hl=en&sa=X&ei=xE0TT-fyGLGG0QGXm7CZAw&ved=0CDMQ6AEwAQ#v=onepage&q=au%20and%20gnau%20gifting&f=false

[10] www.cooperationcommmons.com/node/358

[11] *Outliers* by Malcolm Gladwell published by Little, Brown and Company November 18, 2008

[12] *International Marketing 2 Canadian Edition.* Philip R. Cateora, John L. Graham, Nicolas Papdopolous. 2008. Mcgraw- Hill Ryerson

[13] *Cross Cultural Gift Giving Etiquette*, Kwintessential

[14] http://en.wikipedia.org/wiki/Dowry#In_Europe

[15] *Why the West Rules--for Now: The Patterns of History, and What They Reveal About the Future.* By Ian Morris. McClelland & Stewart October 2010

[16] http://www.maasai-association.org/maasai.html

[17] Human Planet, *BBC*

[18] http://www.longrangeweather.com/600bc.htm

[19] http://www.sdupdate.org/component/content/article/3-in-brief/117-el-nino-and-increased-risk-for-civil-conflict

[20] *Thought Vibration: Or, the Law of Attraction in the Thought World*, William W. Atkinson, Nabu Press, 2010

[21] http://books.google.ca/books?id=3L0BCCoFMRgC&pg=PA297&lpg=PA297&dq=martin+seligman+chapter+9+authentic+happiness&source=bl&ots=__wPfdiGf6&sig=RKpDvbIMEVIY-lv6P7iH-g3vUb8&hl=en&sa=X&ei=aFITT-udO6Xv0gGEvJSiAw&ved=0CDQQ6AEwAQ#v=onepage&q&f=false

[22] *Maimonides: The Life and World of One of Civilization's Greatest Minds*, Joel L Kraemer, Doubleday Religion, 2008

[23] *Think And Grow Rich*, Napoleon Hill, Tribeca Books, 2011

[24] *Think And Grow Rich*, Napoleon Hill, Tribeca Books, 2011

[25] *The Sugary Secret of Self-Control*, Steven Pinker, The New York Times, September 02, 2011

[26] *Savoring Beliefs Inventory (SBI): A scale for measuring beliefs about savouring* FRED B. BRYANT Loyola University Chicago, Chicago, Illinois, USA

[27] McCullough, M. E., Emmons, R. A., & Tsang, J. (2002). *The grateful disposition: A conceptual and empirical topography*

[28] http://www.revolutionary-war-and-beyond.com/facts-on-thomas-jefferson.html

[29] *A Lincoln*. A Biography Written by Ronald C. White, Jr. Random House. May 2010

[30] *Meditations* (Penguin Classics) [Paperback] by Marcus Aurelius (Author), Martin Hammond (Editor)

[31] *Flourish*, Martin E. P. Seligman, Free Press, 2011

CPSIA information can be obtained at www.ICGtesting.com
Printed in the USA
LVOW122156280612

288153LV00001B/132/P